# PRAISE for

## The Walk – *Reflections on Life and Faith from the Appalachian Trail*

"...uniquely informative and inspirational...a must have for those who seek spiritual insight while in the wilderness. Windtalker and Mom share pictures of the peaks and valleys of their trail experiences as well as the wisdom they gained during their adventure. You will find treasures in every chapter."

- **Craig and Suzy Miles** - Founders, Appalachian Trail Servants, Inc. & Authors of, *Seeker's Guide to the Spiritual Wilderness*

"...a very good book written by two very good people. Randy and Georgia do not write as "armchair philosophers" – sitting on the sidelines of life spouting nice sounding but empty spiritual platitudes... they write from the nitty-gritty of personal (and sometimes painful) real world experience...a masterful job...through memorable stories and thoughtful use of scripture, they show how their journey on the A.T. closely mirrors our journey with God...The parallels between "trail life" and "real life" spirituality are skillfully drawn and easily understood...equally accessible both to those who might consider themselves beginners on their spiritual journey and those who have been journeying with Christ for many years. Both will discover the ring of truth in these pages. And both will be encouraged – and equipped – to travel well the trail before them."

- **Ken Jackson,** Pastor of Spiritual Formation, Cedarbrook Community Church, Clarksburg, MD

"...an insightful book that weaves experiences on the Appalachian Trail, Native American wisdom, and scripture into an enjoyable, spiritual read...describes the challenge, beauty and wonder of the A.T. from Randy and Georgia's perspective as thru- hikers...inspires the reader by relating those footsteps to the challenges of our daily lives, and more specifically, to our walk of faith...I found a trail of tales and challenges, bits of wisdom, guiding scripture and devotionals that stopped me in my tracks and made me evaluate where I am in my walk...this book may lead you to Maine or Georgia, or somewhere in between to start your own walk."

- **Nick Melnick**, Worship Leader and Hiker

"...Windtalker and Mom demonstrate the life-affirming possibilities of adventure for persons of any age. The value of planning, enduring, accomplishing and celebrating a challenging dream shines through as they share the lessons they learned together as thru-hikers on the Appalachian Trail."

**- The Rev. Barbara J. Curtis,** First United Methodist Church, Warrensburg, Missouri

"...gives readers a wonderful opportunity to learn valuable lessons from Scripture through the many adventures they encountered on their A.T. thru-hike...lessons are easy to learn and understand because they were captured in the midst of the real life experiences on the trail!"

**- Mathew McCabe,** Youth Pastor, Cedarbrook Community Church, Clarksburg, Maryland

"...a wonderful book. Each chapter gives you a reflective devotional and thoughtful prayer at the end. A wonderful tool!...exciting and breathtaking journal entries...Wonderful lessons to soak in...Heartfelt trail angel stories that demonstrate the love for mankind that still exists...a wonderful account of the simple things that God gives us, vistas to experience, joys of the little things that add such pleasure to our lives...encourages us to seek out the visible and familiar signs of God's presence....points out the benefits of simplicity ...The last chapter, "Pride & Humility," is an awesome read for everyone, a life lesson to certainly meditate on....an inspiring book recommended to everyone, life lessons for all, with wonderful scripture quoted form the Bible that reminds us that God is in control and without Him, nothing is possible..."

**- Cathy Benton,** A.T. Section Hiker

"As an occasional A.T. hiker and a "thru-hike dreamer", I was skeptical of how Randy and Georgia were going to be able to put the sights, sounds and emotions of the A.T. into words. However, I was pleasantly surprised as their words came, as close as words can, in capturing the beauty that surrounded their thru-hike. Matching those words with their own humility, makes their life lessons even more valuable."

**- Gina McCabe,** Administrative Assistant, Metro American Volleyball Club

# The Walk

*Reflections on Life and Faith from the Appalachian Trail*

Randy Motz & Georgia Harris

# The Walk

## Reflections on Life and Faith from the Appalachian Trail

Copyright © 2010 by Randy A. Motz & Georgia L. Harris
The Qualtech Resource Group, Inc.

First Edition

Printed in the United States of America.

Cover Design: Randy Motz, The Qualtech Resource Group, Inc.
Front and Back Cover Photos: Georgia L. Harris

For information, or to order additional copies of this book, contact:

The Qualtech Resource Group, Inc.
Germantown, MD 20874
www.QualtechResourceGroup.com
or
www.CreateSpace.com

ISBN: 1449940773
EIN-13: 9781449940775

The Walk                                        Table of Contents

# Acknowledgements

As with any worthwhile endeavor, nothing can be successfully accomplished without the help of many friends, family and associates—this book is no exception. We wish to thank Roger and Mary Ellen Franks who first asked us about the spiritual aspects of our hike after we returned home. Our gratitude also goes out to the churches where we initially shared the message of spiritual lessons from the trail – they motivated us to talk through and refine the key points we have identified as chapters in this book.

To the many capable and loving people who reviewed and edited this book, Ken Jackson, Mathew and Gina McCabe, David and Barbara Curtis, Craig and Suzy Miles, Cathy Benton and Nick Melnick, we offer our heartfelt thanks. Your editorial and spiritual contributions were extremely insightful and helped us more clearly reflect on what we wanted to say and to evaluate how we could best reach our intended audience.

To my hiking partner, best fried, and loving wife, Georgia, go my personal thanks for creating the outline for this work, researching and selecting Scriptural content and other suitable references, composing the devotionals, as well as editing, editing, and editing. Thanks for pushing me to stay focused on writing and avoid being distracted by the busyness of life. You are my biggest critic and most loyal fan.

Most especially, Georgia and I wish to thank God for giving us the opportunity to hike the Appalachian Trail where we came to better know and understand Him. Thank you for blessing us with the passion, gifts and the talents to communicate what a walk of faith is like through the words in this book.

We dedicate this book to our parents and our children from whom we receive so much love, strength, encouragement and inspiration. It is to you that we wish to pass on our understanding of faith and how it influences our lives. May what we learned about faith and life on the Appalachian Trail help you make your journey through life all that you dreamed it would be and all that God intended to be.

Life is a fascinating journey, a wondrous labyrinth of unforeseen circumstances, opportunities, challenges, consequences, relationships and enlightenment. Along the journey are countless opportunities to experience and learn: to laugh, to cry, to fear, to overcome, to love, to feel anger, and to grow as human beings, each in our own unique way. There are also moments when, despite our best intentions and efforts, we lose our way. The twists and turns of our existence take us down paths where we sometimes find ourselves lost and searching for the way back to where we were intended to travel. Hopefully, those misguided excursions are brief, leaving no lasting ill effects, and we learn valuable life-lessons from them—lessons that allow us to return to the path of life we were once on with a greater understanding of ourselves. This myriad of unique experiences, and how we react to and embrace them, defines who we are or who we will become. It is up to each of us to make the most of our own journey and develop our own sense of self and purpose. We each set goals for our lives and strive to reach those goals by using life's experiences, both positive and negative, as a map. In many respects, life's remarkable pilgrimage is not all that different from backpacking the Appalachian Trail.

For us, "Windtalker" and "Mom," the trail names that we adopted prior to our thru-hike, our walk from Georgia to Maine was to be a straightforward exercise in character building and physical endurance. It was a self-imposed challenge intended to help us escape the proverbial "rat race" we were mired in, allowing our souls to take a deep, cleansing breath of freedom, and help us refocus our priorities. Those six months of walking, carrying everything we needed on our backs and with only each other to rely upon, became a microcosm of the sum total of our previous life experiences. But, it was not long after beginning our journey that we came to the realization that this adventure was much more than simply a quest for self-fulfillment. There was something much larger, more important, more enduring, and more engaging happening within each of us. Traveling the 2,175 miles of the Appalachian Trail, surrounded by the wonders of creation and finding a peaceful sanctuary in the solitude of the wilderness, opened up a world of fresh perspectives on our "journey of life." And not unlike the path of our lives, the trail provided a distinct blend of breathless anticipation, fear of the unknown, the wonder of discovery and the joy of the realized. Overcoming each new challenge brought with it a lesson that we could carry with us for a lifetime and every new experience added an entirely new dimension to how we viewed the world and ourselves. As our days on the trail slowly shifted from winter to spring, then through summer and into fall, we discovered we were not alone on this modern-day vision quest.

The reasons our fellow thru-hikers gave for being on the A.T. were as varied as their hometowns and their personalities. But, flowing beneath each explanation for their own quest for identity by thru-hiking the A.T. was the true, if unspoken, purpose for their journey. The real motive seemed to

---

## Native American Wisdom

*"My mother was a good woman. I thought she was the wisest person in the whole world. So one day—when I was just a little feller, maybe six or seven—I asked her how I could become wise like her. She just laughed and laughed and said I was awfully young to ask such questions. But, she said, since I asked, she would tell me.*

*'Life is like a path,' she said, smiling down at me, 'and we all have to walk the path. If we live through the night, we have to get up and start walking down that path again. As we walk down that path we'll find experiences like little scraps of paper in front of us along the way. We must pick up those pieces of scrap paper and put them in our pockets. Every single scrap of paper we come to should be put in our pockets. Then, one day, we will have enough scraps of paper to put together and see what they say. Maybe we will have enough to make some sense. Read the information and take it to heart. Then put the pieces back in that pocket and go on, because there will be more pieces to pick up. Later we can pull them out and study them and maybe learn a little more. If we do this all through life, we'll know when to pull out those scraps to read more of the message. The more we read, the more we'll learn the meaning of life. We can become wise—or at least wiser than we were.' She said, 'But, if we never pick up those scraps of paper and never read them, we'll never become wiser. We'll keep on wondering about life and never learn the Creator's instructions.'"* [1] - Uncle Frank Davis, Pawnee

---

be one of a spiritual nature—a search for life's meaning and direction.

There were those fresh out of college who wanted to use their hike as a way to postpone their headlong rush into the chaos and obligations of working society for as long as possible. Alive with youthful exuberance, being on the trail provided a prolonged opportunity for them to sort through all they had learned in college and to weigh its relevance in light of what they were currently learning on the trail. It was their "swan song" to adolescence. It was also a time to see if they actually were who they believed they were. Then, with their "everything is possible" approach to life, they could use their trail revelations to set their life's compass and decide what their next life move would be. The spiritual overtones of their adventure on the A.T. were undeniable.

> *"It were as well to be educated in the shadow of a mountain as in more classic shade. Some will remember, no doubt, not only that they went to college but that they went to the mountain."* – Henry David Thoreau (engraved on a rock on Mt. Greylock in Massachusetts)

For some, hiking was an escape from the emotional impact of a failed relationship, as was the case with one of our hiking companions. His spiritual journey was one made in order to try to make sense out of the senseless, resolve the anger and despair he was feeling and to joyously, if fearfully, move on with his life. Whether his journey of enlightenment and a return to some semblance of emotional stability was successful, only he would know. But, what he might learn about himself in the process of his hike could become a source of strength he could draw from in the future.

Then, there were those whose very existence relied on being on the A.T. for as long as possible. For them, the trail offered a safe and stress-free alternative to the pressures and demands of society. The trail provided a haven from the other harsh realities of "the real world." Every day spent on the trail was a day spent on a journey swathed in solitude, searching for peace, and communing with the wonders of nature surrounding them Their forays into society were few and brief, often only long enough to resupply before heading back to the trail. They seemed to rely on the wilderness to keep them emotionally grounded and spiritually afloat, while the world around them was dealing with the onslaught of multiple priorities, ever-evolving technology, and shifting economic and moral sands.

Finally, there were those like us—those who had spent the better part of their lives toiling in corporate America, raising families, buying and selling homes, and ultimately coming to the realization, with retirement looming on the horizon, that there had to be more to the American Dream than we had been led to believe. Hiking the A.T. was a chance to pursue a different dream—one that posed unique challenges and the possibility of exhilarating rewards. A dream that required us to call up every ounce of fortitude we possessed and to draw upon every past experience we had lived through in order to make that dream a reality. Little did we know that the pursuit of this dream would also open up a world of spiritual understanding beyond our wildest musings.

No matter who we were or where we had come from, this prolonged journey in the wilderness forced all of us to slow down our lives. It freed our souls and imaginations to wonder, dream, dance, and once again believe in the unbelievable. Being on the trail also allowed us the freedom to spend time looking into our souls to reflect on the victories and defeats, friends and enemies, successes and mistakes, and to finally make sense of life, to discover how we fit into our unique destiny.

Mom and I have been involved in church ministries for many years, she in teaching and leadership roles, and me in music. Yet, we had not given any real thought to the spiritual nature our own hike might take on. Nevertheless, it was not long after beginning our sojourn that the parallels between our thru-hike and a walk of faith became obvious. With each turn of the trail, each view from a ridgeline and with each person we encountered, the similarities became just too unmistakable to ignore. Our hike became a metaphor for our lives, for just as in life, we encountered spiritual lessons with every new experience on the trail. It was then that we cast aside the act of simply traveling by foot, in awe of all that surrounded us, and instead focused on what we could learn about a walk of faith within the context of our hike.

As we walked, we spent time reflecting on, and discussing, how we could make a difference in people's lives along the trail and in society. Our conundrum was that, because we were in such unfamiliar surroundings, we were not sure just how we might make a lasting impact on the trail. We labored over numerous ideas, but none seemed to fit who we are nor did they seem to use the gifts and talents we had been given. It was not until we arrived home after completing our adventure that this aspect of our life-changing undertaking became clear to us. The number one question asked of us while we were trail, when people discovered that we were married, was, *"So how are you getting along?"* We were constantly confounded by people's amazement over our response that, despite the rigors of the trail and being together 24/7, our relationship was flourishing and we were having the time of our lives. Moreover, our mention of the fact that thru-hiking the A.T. was Mom's idea garnered more than its share of astonished looks. Could what we learned about each other, our marriage and our future, because of our thru-hike, benefit other couples—be they fellow hikers or merely those looking for some type of relevant guidance for their own relationships? It was from this revelation of purpose that we wrote, *"Solemates – Lessons on Life, Love and Marriage from the Appalachian Trail,"* that tells of our journey from the perspective of the unique challenges and rewards of thru-hiking the A.T. as a married couple. Apparently, one reason for being on the trail was to provide us with the experiences, wisdom, understanding and the passion necessary to counsel others in their relationships.

However, even after completing that book, we still believed there was an even greater purpose for us undertaking such an endeavor as conquering the Appalachian Trail. Each time we returned to the wilderness, to again soak in the natural beauty in every direction, there was always a mystical urging within us that said there was something more we could do with what we learned from our time on the trail. As we thought more deeply about what made our journey the life-transforming event it was, the answer became crystal clear—hiking the Appalachian Trail is an easy-to-understand analogy for one's spiritual journey and the trail itself serves as a metaphor for life. The manifestation of our epiphany, the real reason for our months in the wilds, is the book you are holding in your hands. We do not know whether we made a difference in people's lives while we were on the A.T., but we hope we can do so now with this book; whether you are a hiker or someone simply searching for more a relative way of understanding what it means to walk in faith.

Contained on the pages of this book is a blend of Scripture passages, famous quotes and stories pulled from our experiences on the A.T., as well as from the lives of those who have been forever changed by their faith. There are also many quotes and stories from Native Americans—profound and endearing wisdom handed down from generation to generation that illustrates their spiritual connection with both their Creator and the earth. All these elements have been brought together to explain and support a particular theme, such as prayer, perseverance, faith and service and are designed to point out the unmistakable similarities between being on the trail and a life built on spiritual faith.

Whether you have thru-hiked the Appalachian Trail or have just partaken of its beauty during a section hike, an overnight, or a simple day hike, the parallels with one's journey through life are inescapable. Both are journeys defined by personal dreams and goals, frustration with goals and expectations unmet, joy, pain, anger, hope and love—as well as intimate and oftentimes life-changing encounters with the unexpected. Interwoven within this tapestry of the parallels between life and hiking, is yet another correlation—that of the spiritual. The walk of faith through life is not all that different from hiking the Appalachian Trail; in fact, the experiences of thru-hiking the A.T. possess a spiritual nature of their own.

*"True appreciation of life, and understanding one's self, comes from being embraced by the wonders of nature—not through the cacophony and crush of civilization. Natural beauty is the lifeblood of the spirit and is the food that nourishes and renews the soul. It allows you to see the world anew with childlike eyes, able to see the entire world at once, drawing you ever closer to the Creator."* – Windtalker

*"We all walk a path in our life experience. If we are diligent and lucky and we receive and interpret the signs that are given to us correctly, we find the path that we were meant to be on instead of taking a wrong turn and ending up on the wrong path."* - Mr. Prophet

*"We were nearing the end of another long, hot June day—a day not unlike many others we had experienced over the last month or so. The humidity pressed down on us with such intensity that we were inhaling as much moisture as we were air and our beleaguered bodies were beginning to show the telltale signs of incapacitating fatigue. Twilight caressed the nearby mountains, leaving the trees little more than silhouettes against the pink and orange sky. Despite the oppressive heat, the anticipation of cool drinking water and the soothingly melodious sounds of the stream that awaited us at our destination for the night, Antietam Shelter, put a lilt in our steps. We had walked this particular section of trail before and, having navigated our way along the A.T. now for a little over three months, we were quite confident in our ability to follow the trail to our evening's retreat. However, this confidence was accompanied by complacency, a lack of attention to watching for the white blazes marking our way, and this complacency soon got us into trouble.*

*On the way from Ensign Cowell Shelter in Maryland, and into Pennsylvania, the A.T. crosses several roads, some small gravel affairs and some paved, multi-lane, high-speed, state-maintained drag strips. These highways pose a serious threat to hikers. Weighed down with loaded backpacks makes running a bit awkward and the sight of a backpacker hightailing across a road is reminiscent of a portly porcupine waddling through tall grass. Additionally, spending months walking at 2 to 3 miles per hour—which affects the ability to judge any speed higher than that—makes negotiating the way across a highway full of speeding cars a somewhat perilous endeavor. Exiting from the woods at Old Rte. 16, we looked across to the other side in search of what direction the trail took. For some reason, our memory of the last time we had been this way now completely eluded us. Perhaps the heat and the fatigue were playing games with us.*

*We waited as the intermittent, yet precarious, flow of traffic whizzed by and gazed upon what we took to be the trail on the other side. Each passing car cooled us with a refreshing breeze—a breeze that also mercifully blew away the legion of gnats that had been assailing us all afternoon. Despite seeing no obvious blazes, we were certain the large cut in the woods on the other side of the road was the right way because the path was so wide and well trodden. We quickly made our way across the highway and began our trek up a long, gentle, conifer-lined ascent up into the woods. So confident were we that we were going the right way, we neglected to look for blazes and therefore failed to notice that there were none. After a half-hour of blindly making our way north, nonchalantly chatting all the way, we began to sense that something was amiss. The trail no longer looked like what we had been used to seeing. Even with the dampness of the treadway under foot, we did not see any telltale boot prints from other hikers. It was then that we began a frantic search for blazes and to our dismay found none. Still, we decided to continue forward in the hope that some would miraculously appear. After another several minutes, still having not seen those familiar white, 2-inch by 6-inch marks that are the trademarks of the A.T., it was time to make a decision. We sheepishly and begrudgingly admitted to each other that we had gone the wrong way and the only solution to this faux pas was to head back to the road and locate the correct trail.*

*By now we were even more physically exhausted and the realization that we had erred, and were still a long way from our destination for the night, only added to our exasperation. There was no finger pointing, for the predicament brought on by our decision to follow what we thought was the right path had been a mutual one. Even so, our nerves were frayed and our attitudes were bordering on irascible. We could not escape feeling demoralized by our mistake. After another long thirty minutes, we were again at the edge of the road and began our search for the blazes that escaped our view earlier. Mom headed one direction along the roadside and I the other. I had not walked ten feet when there, laying in the dense underbrush on the embankment, overlooking a cesspool of murky water and assorted trash eight feet below, was a rotted wooden post with two blazes on it, one above the other—the universal sign that the trail was changing direction."* - Windtalker & Mom

This experience provided us with a valuable lesson. We had allowed our egos to dictate the direction of our journey and we had paid dearly for it, both physically and emotionally. What was more exasperating was that, after our ill-fated sojourn, we reviewed our trail map and guide book and found the direction we should have gone clearly indicated in both. From that point forward, when no blazes were evident, and we were in doubt of which direction to go, we would never again forego using the trail information readily at hand and simply rely on our presumptions of which way was correct.

Is how we make poor decisions and the consequences we suffer on our *trail of life* any different? Often, despite what life has already taught us, and the information readily at hand, we become overly self-assured, even lazy, and disregard life's "blazes" in lieu of our own brash belief in what is the correct direction. In our case, we had forgone relying on our past experience on this section of the A.T. and the guidance of our trail data book. We allowed our vanity to take over and, as in real life, the result was a learning experience—one with an unpleasant price.

Humans have been endowed with an internal moral compass, an innate sense of right and wrong, "a conscience," that ultimately affects every decision we make. When heeded, this sense of direction helps us stay on our life's course. It is also a sense that nags at our soul whenever we make less-than-wise decisions—erroneous choices made despite every ounce of information, intuition, and common sense we possess. This uniquely human characteristic is often pushed into the recesses of our psyches when we are presented with options that seemingly offer us an easier, or more attractive, route to personal satisfaction. We also purposely throw circumspection to the winds and allow our egos to blur the edges of good judgment in direct contradiction to what our conscience is telling us. No matter how hard we try, that innate sense of right and wrong will not allow us to interminably rationalize our wrong decisions. We cannot overcome that visceral nagging that affirms that we chose incorrectly and that we will eventually suffer some type of consequence—even if it is nothing more than our own self-loathing. Every attempt to feign knowing better or insisting that the guidance given to us was bogus, or outdated, only makes matters worse. It is the very weight of our conscience, the response of our moral compass, which forces us to re-evaluate our decisions, regain our sense of direction, and gently persuades us to backtrack along our ill-chosen path. Then, with confidence and a clear conscience, we can move forward in the right direction.

To put this human dynamic into hiking terms, many a veteran hiker, when becoming lost, relies on the over-arching drive of ego—continuing forward and believing that years of hiking experience will miraculously correct the error. The truth is that most search and rescue missions in the wilderness are the result of this very type of prideful mistake. Rather than admit the folly of their ways, lost hikers rely on their own devices, throwing all logic and conscience to the wind, and walk further into potential peril. Had they accepted the mistake as part of the adventure, rather than letting it impinge upon the pride they take in their level of wilderness expertise, they would have backtracked to the last recognizable place on the trail. From there, they could find the correct trail—or path—and continue on to their predestined goal.

In September, as we sat with a group of our hiking friends at the Hurd Brook Shelter, a few miles before our climactic climb up Mt. Katahdin, we all began to reminisce about our respective journeys thus far. Around a campfire, everyone expressed the bittersweet emotions they were feeling over the forthcoming ascent of Mt. Katahdin. Their sincerity flowed forth with a clarity and honesty that brought us all even closer together as a "trail family." During those conversations, the subject of getting lost or traveling the wrong direction suddenly came up and "Sumo" began to expound upon his experience going around one of the many lakes that adorn the mountaintops in Maine. He spoke of reaching an intersection on the trail, near the lake's edge, where he saw no white blazes. What he did see though, going around one side of the lake, was a trail made quite distinct by the multitude of muddy footprints stretching as far as the eye could see. Believing that if that many hikers had taken this route before him, he could set out confident he was going the right way. It was not until some time later that he began to see blue blazes indicating he was on a side-trail that had left the A.T. He told of how he decided to continue anyway, hoping this blue-blaze trail would reunite with the A.T. on the far side of the lake, which thankfully it did. He considered himself fortunate to have found his way back to the correct trail, but freely admitted to the frustration of having wasted a great deal of time and energy going the wrong way. And what of the wonders he missed by taking the wrong path? In retrospect, he realized that simply because so many others took a certain path did not mean it was the right path. In life as on the trail, one needs to be following the blazes laid out before them. Simply because so many others have gone a certain way does not mean it is the correct way.

Life's journey is also filled with unexpected trials and rewards, wrong turns and miscues, pain and joy, surprises and, yes, even the mundane. Though our goal of reaching Mt. Katahdin was quite clear, life's goals are often nebulous—open to reinterpretation, revision, refinement, development, and metamorphosis. Whatever original life goals we set for ourselves, those goals invariably fall victim to circumstance, chance, destiny, knowledge gained, understanding acquired, and a maturation of our personalities. Life becomes a trail with infinite detours and ubiquitous intersections. Without a sense of direction, or the guiding wisdom of one who has already traveled that trail, the journey of life can leave you wandering far from what you set out to accomplish. Without the knowledge and understanding of what is the "right path," the temptation to take a seemingly more direct, or easier, route can leave you totally lost and in need of rescue. What you generally find is that the easy way is seldom the right way.

> *"Your word is a lamp to my feet and a light for my path."* - Psalm 119:105 (NIV)

Living on the Appalachian Trail for up to six months supplied more than the realization of a dream—the completion of a grand and momentous adventure. There is something unquestionably "spiritual" about this particular journey. Being an integral part of the delicate, yet unyielding, fabric of nature, wandering through rich forests and fertile valleys, standing atop windswept mountain peaks and balds, and challenging the forces of nature that assail you each day, provide a sense of awe and wonder that cannot be denied. The overwhelming sense that you are part of something much bigger than yourself envelops you like a thick morning fog. Evidence of the spiritual is all around you and taking the time to see it, feel it, hear it, breathe it, and acknowledge its influence in your life bestows upon you a new understanding of what is truly important in life and the role you play in creation. Yet, even off the trail, life still presents moments of spiritual wonder if we simply take the time to notice and acknowledge them. For those whose lives rush forward without the understanding of the spiritual underpinnings of every experience, the journey of life can be a long and unrewarding one.

As soon as you step foot on the A.T., there are the white blazes painted on trees, rocks, and posts to keep you on the correct path. On the mountain tops there even piles of rocks, called cairns, that reassure you of your direction, whether in bright sunshine or in the fog and clouds that often obscure your view of the trail

> ### Native American Wisdom
> *"Everything is laid out for you. Your path is straight ahead of you. Sometimes it's invisible but it's there. You may not know where it is going, but still you have to follow the path. It's the path of the Creator. That's the only path there is."* [2] – Leon Shenandoah (Six Nations Iroquois Confederacy)

ahead. In order to successfully complete a thru-hike, you have to follow the white blazes and cairns. In spiritual terms, to complete your journey of faith, you need to follow the path set forth in the Bible— God's trail guide for life. It is often easy to get lost on the A.T. because the blazes are sometimes faded. Many road crossings, as we discovered, have poor markings. An intersection in life can be equally confusing without some indication of which is the right way to go. As Sumo discovered, sometimes others in front of you have worn a path down the wrong way, which has you believing you are on the correct path. Life is no different. But if you follow where Jesus leads and not where other people have gone, no matter how right other paths may seem, you will always remain on the right path.

*"There is a way that seems right to a man, but in the end it leads to death."* – Proverbs 16:25 (NIV)

More often than not, the trail is extremely difficult—it may be narrow and hard to see, and sometimes even animal trails look like the path. There sometimes are moments when you are not sure you see the trail at all. Yet, you put your faith in the blazes and cairns and in your guidebook and maps, and fearlessly trudge on. The narrow trail becomes a challenge of your will, your skill, and your faith. It is a challenge that bestows its rich reward upon you when you persevere and finally reach the next glorious mountaintop, bald, or frosty meadow glistening in the morning sun. This same type of challenge awaits you on your walk of faith and the rewards of pushing on are eternal. There will be innumerable times when you will not be sure where the correct path is and a walk of faith may also seem confusing, difficult, directionless, or obscured by the overgrowth of life.

*"But small is the gate and narrow the road that leads to life, and only a few find it." –* Mathew 7:14 (NIV)

Others, who are following a more obvious, and seemingly more rewarding and enjoyable route, will become a source of temptation—a temptation to follow them instead of Jesus. It is during those times that only a steadfast faith and a determination to follow the guidebook given to you by God, will keep you going—going in the right direction on the correct path.

Sometimes the trail can be very lonely. Mom and I always had each other for company but there were still many days when we longed for the companionship of our fellow hikers. The path of faith may also be lonely at times. Overwhelmed by the immensity of the task you have undertaken, or confused by a fork in the trail, you will long for companionship, a reassuring voice and a word of encouragement or some sage advice. Remember that you are never alone on your walk of faith—God is there to keep you company, to keep you safe and assuage your doubts and fears. You may not hear his voice but he hears even your thoughts.

There is an old legend regarding a Cherokee youth's rite of passage that dramatically illustrates this point. When he is young, a Cherokee boy is taken by his father into the forest where he is blindfolded and left alone. He is required to sit on a stump the whole night and not remove the blindfold until the rays of the morning sun shine through it. He cannot cry out for help to anyone. Once he survives the night, he is a MAN. He cannot tell the other boys of this experience, because each lad must come into manhood on his own.

The boy is naturally terrified. He can hear all kinds of noises and he believes that wild beasts must surely be all around him. Maybe even some human might do him harm. The wind blows the grass and earth, shaking his stump, but he sits stoically, never removing the blindfold. It is the only way he can become a man.

Finally, after a horrific night, the sun appears and he removes his blindfold. It is then that he discovers his father sitting on the stump next to him. He had been at watch the entire night, protecting his son from harm.

We, too, are never alone. Even when we do not know it, God is watching over us, sitting on the stump beside us.

*"When you pass through the waters,*
*I will be with you;*
*and when you pass through the rivers,*
*they will not sweep over you.*
*When you walk through the fire,*
*you will not be burned;*
*the flames will not set you ablaze."* – Isaiah 43:2 (NIV)

Many days, as Mom and I trudged along windy ridgelines in dense fog, sloshed across endless cornfields in lightning and pouring rain, or meandered through stands of towering pines, we often did not speak to each other for hours. Even when we did talk, our conversations were often laconic. There was an emotional harmony and non-verbal communication between us, the result of our intrinsic understanding of each other's needs and desires, joy and pain, fears and hopes. We were content in our thoughts and with our place on this journey knowing we had each other. It is wise to find a close friend in Christ with whom you can share your journey, much as Mom and I shared our A.T. journey. Like our need to be with a group of like-minded trekkers in camp at night, it is good to find a group with which to share and grow.

*"Let us not give up meeting together, as some are in the habit of doing, but let us encourage one another..."* - Hebrews 10:25 (NIV)

When doing a long-distance hike, or any hike for that matter, there are rules of the trail and laws of the wilderness that must be adhered to. Deviating from those rules or underestimating those primeval laws can have dire consequences. Fail to hang your food bag from a tree before nestling into the warmth and security of your sleeping bag and the creatures of night will steal you blind. Drink unfiltered water and you run the risk of contracting Giardia and spending the next several days suffering the ill effects of nausea and diarrhea. In addition, if you disregard the telltale signs of impending bad weather, you could find yourself caught in a lightning storm on a treeless ridgeline with no safe place to hide.

One's journey as a Christian has its own foundational axioms. Much like hiking to a distant and all-encompassing destination, succeeding on one's journey of faith requires the same type of willful adherence to its own mores. If one loses sight of the laws of the trail and ends up lost, reliance on good judgment, skill, and a guide book is the way to locate the correct way again. In a Christian perspective, if one loses his or her way, God's grace and forgiveness offers the way back to the correct path and His words provide the map.

> *"All that passing laws against sin did was produce more lawbreakers. But sin didn't, and doesn't, have a chance in competition with the aggressive forgiveness we call grace. When it's sin versus grace, grace wins hands down. All sin can do is threaten us with death, and that's the end of it. Grace, because God is putting everything together again through the Messiah, invites us into life—a life that goes on and on and on, world without end."* - Romans 5:20-21 (The Message)

On the A.T., there is a term called "yellow blazing" that refers to leaving the trail and taking the quickest route to the next town by hitchhiking or walking along the yellow lines on a road. Those that yellow blaze circumvent many of the trials of the journey for the sake of the short-term reward of quickly reaching the next destination. But in the process of taking a short-cut, they can cheat themselves out of many of the long-term joys and rewards of staying on the trail and experiencing all it has to offer. So many of the most cherished memories of hiking the A.T. are found on the trail, in the valleys, and on the mountaintops—not in the towns. As a Christian, a successful walk of faith does not allow for shortcuts. You must be able to distinguish the difference between long-term rewards and short-term pleasure, for there is no way to *yellow blaze* your Christian walk and still grow. Those long-term rewards bring with them distinct pleasures—one just may have to wait a while to experience them. And because you waited, stayed on the path, and did not try to take a short-cut, the magnitude of that pleasure will be overwhelming and eternal.

> *"Jesus answered, I am the way and the truth and the life. No one comes to the Father except through me."* - John 14:6 (NIV)

In contrast to the yellow blazes that offer short cuts, there are the "blue blazes"—those that guide you to a shelter, water source, or a scenic overlook. They take you to places of rest and the solitude of a retreat. They lead to places to find refreshment, places to view creation, and places to reflect and meditate. After you have experienced all these things, the blue blaze trails always lead back to the main trail. In your walk of faith there are also spiritual equivalents to blue blaze trails—journeys you must daily take to find rest for your soul (a shelter), to reflect and meditate on God's Word—Living Water (a spring) and to understand the nature of his grace (a grand vista). And you can be confident that those spiritual blue blazes will always lead you back to "The Path."

*"Ask where the good way is, and walk in it, and you will find rest for your souls."* - Jeremiah 6:16 (NIV)

You can never complete the Appalachian Trail if you do not first get started. For us, our hike was an all-consuming dream—a desire to undertake and complete a journey that would change our lives forever. Yes, completing the trail was hard and there were days when we wondered if we would really make it. However, we vowed that quitting would not be an option no matter how tired, sore, wet, or frustrated we might become. To finish well, we had to keep going every day and each day we became stronger, more confident, and learned more about others and ourselves. We came to understand life more and gained a greater appreciation for the blessings that were everyday occurrences during our journey. It was, in every sense of the word, a personal spiritual growth process.

To be a Christian you also have to get started and, just like attempting a long-distance hike, a Christian life will be hard. There will be days when your very faith is challenged by the unexpected and the temptation to find an easier way, to yellow blaze, will challenge your will. There will be days when you simply want to leave "The Path" and follow the crowd. But, much like overcoming the grueling, dangerous, and precipitous climb to the ridgeline of a place like Wildcat Mountain, to be rewarded with the indescribable vistas of New Hampshire below, overcoming the challenges of faith that lay before you will also provide you with rewards beyond your ability to comprehend them. For those who choose to walk in faith, life becomes a spiritual growth process—one in which you must always keep your eye on the prize.

*"Don't look for shortcuts to God. The market is flooded with surefire, easygoing formulas for a successful life that can be practiced in your spare time. Don't fall for that stuff, even*

*though crowds of people do. The way to life—to God!—is vigorous and requires total attention."* -    Matthew 7:13-14 (The Message)

As we made our way north, we strove to stay on the right path (trail), tried to avoid getting lost and joyfully labored onward day after day. We gave our all to our journey to Mt. Katahdin—time, finances, health, hearts and souls. Every thought and every fiber of our being was devoted to that one irrepressible goal. Nothing else mattered. One's journey of faith requires exactly the same dedication—nothing more, nothing less.

*"Love the Lord your God with all your heart and with all your soul and with all your mind and with all your strength."*
– Mark 12:30 (NIV)

We pursued our quest to complete the A.T. intentionally, never losing sight of the goal before us. When we reached the summit of Mt. Katahdin on that sunny day in late September, we were overcome with a joy and sense of accomplishment unlike anything we had ever felt before. Those types of feelings are also the hallmarks of a walk of faith. To experience them, your spiritual journey needs to be intentional and all consuming. To accomplish this, you need to sustain focus by reading and meditating on God's Word each day. Those words are the map needed to make it to the ultimate goal. Each of us must take steps every day, no matter how difficult. And as we walk in faith, following the "spiritual blazes" that God has set before us, our joy and sense of accomplishment will also reach its zenith when we hear at the end of your journey,

*".....Well done, my good and faithful servant......"* - Mathew 25:21 (NIV)

---

## Devotional: *"The Path"*

*"Your word is a lamp to my feet and a light for my path."* Psalm 119:105

The parallel between following the blazes and following God's Word were obvious to us on our hikes long before we noted any of the other similarities described in this book. Sometimes, going astray, while trying to stay on the path, as happened on the trail, also happened in my life and on my walk of faith. On the trail, I happened to fall a lot. The same thing has happened in my life, many more times than I like to admit. Failed marriages are quite public. Given that I'm on my third marriage, it's obvious that I've made a few mistakes—that is, I've gotten off the right path.

One of the common struggles of being a Christian is knowing whether you are on the right path and doing the right things with your life. I struggle with several questions. Am I doing what God has planned for my life? How do I know? Am I just seeking after joy and adventure? Am I regularly stopping to reflect on what God would have me choose with my time and energy? When I stop to reflect on His Word, I suspect that all too often I'm looking for excitement and the next big thing. It's easy to get off track! Everything in our culture cries out to just do it and just have fun.

I know that God has given me passions and dreams, gifts and abilities. I also know that I regularly need to take time to read His Word and reflect on who God is, so that I can follow his plans for my life. – *Mom*

## Prayer

*"Lord, thank you for your mercy and grace and for helping me get up when I fall down. Help me focus on your purpose for me so that I walk in the path you have planned for my life."*

*"Prayer draws us near to our own souls."*- Herman Melville,
1849

For those of faith, it is called prayer—a heartfelt request for providence or an expression of thanksgiving. Others call it wishing or hoping—the results of which manifest in good luck or fortuitous coincidence. It has been said, "Even atheists pray in foxholes" and as a thru-hiker, whether your life has a spiritual side or not, there is no denying that at some point on your journey from Georgia to Maine, or as a "southbounder" hiking from Maine to Georgia, you will find yourself praying—mere wishing and hoping is an unsatisfactory substitute. You pray that your knees and feet will stop hurting or that you will find water before you run out on a hot, humid August day. You may even pray that you will make it through Mahoosuc Notch without tragically falling or, as Mt. Katahdin looms in the distance, that you will not get hurt and have to curtail your adventure after traveling so far for so long. You might even find yourself saying a silent prayer of gratitude for the "trail angels" who just provided you with a cold soda and a hamburger or gave you a ride into town so you could rest and take a much-needed shower.

You may fervently believe there is no "god." Nevertheless, when you are on an exposed ridgeline with no place to hide anywhere in sight and lightning, driving rain, and a menacing wind has you questioning your very mortality and sanity, you often react quite differently. Under stressful trail circumstances such as this, where the situation is totally out of your control, and the words "hopelessly doomed" flash through your mind, it is probably safe to say that most look to a power higher than themselves to get safely to the next shelter or campsite. When people face extreme circumstances and realize that their feeble attempts to survive by their own wits and power are not enough, they generally turn to God for help. There were many circumstances such as these during our 2006 thru-hike, but one stands out above all the rest as an example of answered prayer.

*May 7, 2006:*

"This was a day that quickly evolved into one with the potential of being life threatening—of ending our adventure far too early. Were it not for our wilderness first aid training and a "miracle," we could have been in very serious trouble. We woke up to rain which, had it not been for our excitement over the views we would have from Grayson Highlands a few miles ahead, could have easily dampened our enthusiasm over even getting out of our sleeping bags. Thankfully, the rain soon let up so we packed our bags and got going as quickly as we could, though we had the nagging feeling that we had not seen the last of the downpours that had persisted over the last several hours. We were grievously correct in our assumption. The rain did return and, despite becoming mildly damp but still feeling comfortable, we were not going to let a little rain dampen our enthusiasm—that is until we reached the bald at Buzzard Rock on the way up Whitetop Mountain. On our ascent, we met several southbounders coming off the bald who warned us that it was pretty nasty up there and to be prepared. We had been through this type of thing before, so we were not overly concerned about the prospect of having to reach the summit in less-than-ideal conditions. As we started up the bald, the temperature precipitously dropped, from the balmy 50 °F we woke up to, to a frigid 39 °F. The early morning's gentle breeze had now blossomed into a full-blown gale of what we estimated to be 45 to 50 mph. Our trekking poles, once just devices to help us move forward and save our knees, were now planted in the ground on the leeward side of our bodies to act as buttresses to keep the wind from blowing us over. Our rain gear and pack covers, generally impervious to sudden downpours, were suddenly no match for the wind-driven torrent blasting horizontally across the mountainside. The rain was now being pounded right through our clothes, and through our pack covers into our packs. The sound of flapping silnylon, buffeted by the wind, pounded in our ears and our rain gear stung our skin as the gusts tossed it about like a wind-torn sail in a hurricane..

By the time we reached the summit, we were thoroughly soaked and extremely cold. Our gloves, donned in a feeble attempt to keep our hands warm, were now wringing wet and had become utterly useless for their intended purpose. What caused us the greatest concern was that our body temps were falling rapidly and we knew we would not reach our destination for the day, Thomas Knob Shelter. As we hiked down the long descent from the bald to Elk Garden, at VA 600, we both began to lose feeling in our fingers and we knew it was time to seek some type of safe haven. It was a constant struggle to communicate with each other through chattering teeth in order to check on each other's physical and mental status. Our first aid training had taught us the telltale signs of hypothermia, so it was important that we monitor each other to make sure that neither of us was plummeting across the threshold of this life-threatening condition. Each of us, in our own way, was praying that we would make it to safety before our physical condition grew any worse, possibly bringing our A.T. adventure to an abrupt and, quite possibly, tragic end.

After what seemed like an excruciating eternity, we reached the notch of the mountains at Elk Garden—one prayer answered. For a few minutes, the rain let up enough for us to set up our tent in the woods near VA 600. Another prayer answered. In sight of passing cars, we stripped off every bit of wet clothing, a real delight when we were already half-frozen. It was now 34 °F, as we jumped into our sleeping bags to get warm and ride out the storm. It had become quite apparent to us that our day was going to end and Grayson Highlands would have to wait until another day. We also knew, with so much of what we carried now soaking wet, that we needed to call for assistance and get to town where we could dry out and continue warming up.

As anyone who has hiked the length of the A.T. can attest, cell phone service can oftentimes be spotty and much of the time is non-existent. For hours we had no service and doubted that anything had changed that would somehow allow us to make a connection with Mom's parents, Vince and Anita, a.k.a. "V&A," who were providing trail support during our hike and had also gladly taken on the role of trail angels for others on the trail. Mom pulled out her Treo anyway in the hope that another prayer might be answered. She turned it on and amazingly, for a span of only three minutes, she was able to get two bars of cell service and was able to call V&A to come pick us up. V&A also had no cell *service all morning but, at that precise moment when Mom pressed the "send" button, their phone came alive and they were able to take the call. They were quite some distance away and would not be able to reach us for about two hours. We were fine with that fact. We had already begun to warm up and having a few hours to catch a nap was a welcome sidebar to the morning's hazardous events. It was all really a miracle!*

*Several of our friends made it through the storm to Thomas Knob Shelter and were in even worse straits than we were. They needed to get to town as well, and as we later found out as we all shared our adventure of that day, they experienced much the same miracle. One of the guys in their group attempted to call for help but found he had no service. In a fit of anger, brought on we are sure by the bitter cold and the fact that none of them had even a dry sleeping bag to crawl into, tossed the phone across the inside of the shelter to his buddy a short ten feet away. His friend looked at the phone's screen and discovered they now had service, so he was able to make a call to get them rescued. Unfortunately, they still had to backtrack four miles down the mountain to be picked up. When they recounted their tale to us, they jokingly referred to their phone as their 'God Phone.'"* - Windtalker & Mom

As a long-distance backpacker, even if you don't regularly pray yourself, it is quite possible and probably inevitable, that there are people in your life, back at home, who pray every day for your safety and for the success of your journey. For us, a family from our church who, not having any other tangible way of assisting us on our six-month journey, prayed each day that we would not get any blisters. Yes, it was a rather simple and prosaic request to make of the Maker of the Universe, but it was a prayer that was answered. We completed our entire hike without any of the blisters that plagued so many of our fellow hikers. We did our part to minimize the chances for blisters but, as most every thru-hiker knows, that is nearly impossible to accomplish without some divine intervention.

In an interview with the Grand Rapids Press, after his A.T. hike, Ben Reuschel and his parents spoke about how prayer played a part in the his journey.

*"His parents say they spend little time worrying about their son every day. Their salve is prayer and Scripture reading, especially Psalm 91:13-14, which offers a prayer for protection and safety.*

*'A lot of people are including him in their prayers. He gets bathed in prayer in every day,' said Pat Reuschel, his mother.*

*Each day, Ben Reuschel says, he tries to focus on one of his weaknesses and thinks of ways to improve himself. He is doing his annual reading through the Bible and devouring the occasional novel he finds left behind by other hikers on the trail."* [3]

When Mom and I give talks to church groups about the spiritual nature of our thru-hike, we are often asked,

*"How did you pray?"*

*"Did you pray out loud?"*

*"Together?"*

*"Did you pray every day or over meals?"*

*"Did you have daily devotionals and did you pray holding hands or alone?"*

For those whose spiritual lives are centered within the structure of formal religion, these are reasonable questions to ask. But to spend six months of your life, 24/7, surrounded by the sights, sounds and smells of the very creation we have been put here to protect, admire and worship, *formal* styles of praying seem so restrictive, mundane and wholly inadequate.

*"Be still and know that I am God."* - Psalm 46:10 (NIV)

Out on the trail, every waking hour, every step, and every breath you take is a form of prayer that elicits a response from God. Every time you sit on a rock outcropping, gazing at a lush, jade-green valley below and you say,

*"My God, what an awesome sight,"*

or you gaze at a star-filled sky and quietly wonder if you will ever see anything as spectacular as that again, you are in a real way, praying. You are residing in a special *temple*, one that no man, even with all of his creativity, education, skill and technological savvy, can come close to replicating. Whether you realize it or not, with every vocalized or internalized expression of wonder, you are instinctively giving credit where credit is due and it fills you with a sense of peace and amazement. Yes, we prayed every day and our thankfulness for what we were experiencing became a never-ending prayer—prayer that was free of adherence to ritual and with no confining limits.

For us, prayer became a daylong exercise—oftentimes without even realizing it. Our prayers were not always praiseful recognition of the beauty that surrounded us. Oftentimes they were,

*"Oh God, help us through this day!"*

and often we simply prayed for protection and safety. Sometimes we said a quick prayer that a thunderstorm

> ### Native American Wisdom
>
> *"Grandfather, Great Spirit, once more behold me on earth and lean to hear my feeble voice. You lived first, and you are older than all need, older than all prayer. All things belong to you—the two-legged, the four legged, the wings of the air and all green things that live. You have set the powers of the four quarters of the earth to cross each other. You have made me cross the good road, and the road of difficulties and where they cross the place is holy. Day in, day out, forevermore, you are the life of things."* [4] - Black Elk (Oglala Sioux)

would hold off until our tent was set up or until we arrived at a shelter. Our friend, "Old Drum" prayed while walking, lifting up prayer requests he received while on the trail. It was seldom that our prayers were not answered; not always in the way we expected, but answered just the same. It was only in reflection, while enveloped in the quiet of our campsite or on a towering mountain peak, that the answer came to us in a way we never expected.

There were also the times when the answer was so unmistakable and so dramatic, that there was no denying where the answer came from.

*April 14th:*

*"Today was a day for milestones & miracles! As for milestones, we passed the "200 mile mark" on our journey (we are almost to Maine - NOT!) and we hiked to the highest point on the A.T., Clingman's Dome—6,643' high. As for miracles, we began our morning hiking from the shelter up the long, rock-strewn path that often was only as wide as our boots. On either side of us were the remnants of towering trees, stripped bare by the ravages of time and the elements, standing like ghostly grey sentries amidst the deep greens of the forest. A thick blanket of mist and fog wafted across the mountain ahead of us, devouring everything in sight. At times, we could only see several feet in front of us. The cold wind pummeled us and all the other inhabitants of this mountain— the living and the inanimate. We prayed with every step, that this abominable situation would dissipate before we got to Clingman's Dome so we could take in the panoramic vistas from the observation tower there. Miraculously, as we neared the summit, the clouds and fog completely cleared out and we could not only see our destination but also the majesty of the mountains bathed in the morning sun all around us. Incredibly thankful for our good fortune, and giddy with anticipation as we hiked up the final steep grade to the top, we suddenly remembered that it was Good Friday. It was on that day, thousands of years ago, that Christ carried a cross up to Golgotha to His crucifixion and here we were anguishing over our struggle to carry a mere thirty-five-pound pack up a little mountain. It changed our whole perspective on our morning walk and now our packs did not seem quite as heavy. As we were completing our conversation regarding the significance of this day, we looked up to the sky over Clingman's Dome and there, if only briefly, was a cross formed by two thin clouds—the only clouds remaining in the cobalt-blue morning sky. Talk about hearing from God! As we stood on the narrow ridge before Clingman's and those two clouds were carried away into the distance by a now gentle the wind, we were struck by the immenseness of what was below us and just how insignificant we were in relation to the whole landscape. We also realized how blessed were to be a part of it."* - Windtalker & Mom

All along the Appalachian Trail are churches that offer the comfort of their facilities to trail-weary wanderers. They do this not merely out of a love of the trail or their connection with the creation that the trail meanders through, but because of something much deeper—their Christian responsibility to serve those in need. To hikers they provide not only a warm place to sleep, a hot shower and a hot meal. But, with unyielding empathy, they also bestow the power of prayer unto those who request it, as well as to those who do not. The people of these churches understand the power of prayer and relish the opportunity to exercise that power for the protection of all the tired and smelly vagabonds that limp through their doors.

There is Grace Evangelist Lutheran Church in Waynesboro, Virginia, The Presbyterian Church of the Mountain in Delaware Water Gap, Pennsylvania and St. Thomas Episcopal Church in Vernon, New Jersey, just to name a few. Every one of them stands as an icon of the hospitality of people along the A.T. and they exemplify what it means to be a "trail angel," one who provides support and services to hikers.

Not only do the members of the churches along the A.T. bathe the hikers they meet in prayer, but so do many of the hikers themselves. These churches become a repository of prayers by hikers, for hikers and about hikers. For instance, at churches like St. John's Episcopal Church in Harpers Ferry, West Virginia, many hikers leave prayer requests, not for themselves, but for others.

*"Please pray for "Little Bear" and "Turtle Fast," who just received news that his father passed away unexpectedly at age 57 of organ failure. May they find comfort in the promise of our Lord."* [5]

*Another hiker asks, "Please pray for those who struggle with depression, anxiety, and other mental disorders. May they find solace in the Lord."* [6]

St. John's is located near the Appalachian Trail Conservancy Headquarters, the *psychological halfway point* of the A.T. It holds a beloved place in the history of the trail and in the hearts of all those hikers who pass through its doors because of its ministry to Appalachian Trail hikers. As part of that ministry, St. John's hands out copies of the following prayer to those who stop in for water and to rest.

## Prayer for Appalachian Trail Hikers

*May the angels of the Lord camp around you,*
*And may you commit your way to the Lord.*
*May you walk in integrity,*
*Sure as the feet of deer in high places.*
*May you know in your heart*
*That all the paths of the Lord are mercy and truth.*
*May you be led beside still waters,*
*As well as along rocky paths.*
*May the Lord make your mountain stand strong,*
*And be your rock and your fortress.*
*May he strengthen your heart,*
*And teach you his paths.*
*May God be your salvation and glory,*
*And may you find water when you are thirsty.*
*May you finish your journey in peace,*
*And live in the habitation where his honor dwells.* [7]

The prayers offered by the trail's churches go out to everyone. It does not matter whether a hiker is a Christian or not. The prayers are sincere, visible, and selfless outpourings of love, compassion and encouragement that travel with each wandering soul as they leave the church and head back onto the trail. Their prayers are as vital to a hiker's success and well-being as is water, food and a tent. The churches along the A.T. stand as a glowing tribute to the "One" who teaches all of us to care for one another.

The opportunities to offer up prayers of thanksgiving or need are often crowded out by the hustle and bustle of everyone's *real lives*. The pandemonium associated with surviving in a society mired in the constant rush to meet the next deadline, of getting the kids to their next activity, or simply trying to get ahead, makes it difficult, if not seemingly impossible, to make prayer part of a daily ritual. In addition, the cultural and technological cacophony inherent in our day-to-day living, the cell phones, iPods, computers, and flat-screen TVs, drown out the whispers of our Creator into our soul. In a society that moves so quickly that it only has time for sound bites of information, momentary flashes of images spliced together into video clips that entice our base senses, rather than stimulate our intellect, and the obsession to be constantly *plugged in*, leaves us little time or inclination to connect with the true source of our humanity. But out on the trail, in the reverent solitude of the wilderness, deliberately cut off from all that chaos and unencumbered by electronic paraphernalia, there is nothing but quiet. The chances to hear that still, small voice around every corner, in every valley and on top of every mountain are ever-present and undeniable. The very solitude of the trail allows for a free flow of communication with the Creator of everything around you and his presence is unmistakable—and oftentimes overwhelming.

For those who have undertaken the life-changing challenge of thru-hiking the A.T., and who are also taking the life-changing journey that is a *walk of faith*, the power of prayer is a necessary piece of "gear" for both. Without it, the chances for succeeding at either are slim. In your walk of faith, prayer is a metaphor for water. If you try hiking

> ## Native American Wisdom
>
> *"When we want wisdom we go up on the hill and talk to God. Four days and four nights without food and water. Yes, you can talk to God up on a hill by yourself. You can say anything you want. Nobody's there to listen to you. That's between you and God and nobody else. It's a great feeling to talk to God. I know, I did it way up on the mountain. The wind was blowing. It was dark. It was cold. And I stood there and talked to God."* [8] - Mathew King (Lakota)

the entire trail with no water, at some point you just have to give up because you no longer have the strength or resourcefulness to continue. The weakness of your body flows into your soul and your spirit dies. Your walk of faith is no different and prayer becomes your *living water*.

Each day on the trail offers up endless opportunities for prayer, be they formal or not. Take advantage of those opportunities, relish them, and share them with others. Be a living witness to others and perhaps, with prayer and the sharing of the sights, sounds and moments that are unique to the Appalachian Trail, they too will come to realize how a life of faith will change their life—just like the trail can change their life.

> *"Do not be anxious about anything, but in everything, by prayer and petition, with thanksgiving, present your requests to God."* - Philippians 4:6 (NIV)

One day, high above the clouds on a windy ridgeline in New Hampshire, we stopped to take a break and soak in the amazement of the fall landscape stretched out on either side of the mountain. Ahead, we could see the trail snaking its way up and down, from ridge to ridge, for what seemed like ten miles. Our immediate reaction, aside from that of absolute astonishment at the rugged expanse of mountains ahead of us, was that we were suddenly very tired. Months of walking, sometimes twelve hours a day, had finally caught up to us and we were in need of some divine intercession. Two other thru-hikers, a married couple with the trail names of "Brownie" and "Souleman," suddenly appeared and sat down beside us. They too, bemoaned the fact that they were exhausted and wondered if they would make it to Maine. Then Mom asked them if they had ever heard the story of Moses and the battle with the Amalekites. Brownie believed she had heard it once but could not recount the details, so Mom began to tell us all the biblical tale of how Moses ingeniously overcame fatigue so that he could continue to pray.

> *"Moses ordered Joshua: "Select some men for us and go out and fight Amalek. Tomorrow I will take my stand on top of the hill holding God's staff."*
>
> *Joshua did what Moses ordered in order to fight Amalek. And Moses, Aaron, and Hur went to the top of the hill. It turned out that whenever Moses raised his hands, Israel was winning, but whenever he lowered his hands, Amalek was winning. But Moses' hands got tired. So they got a stone and set it under him. He sat on it and Aaron and Hur held up his hands, one on each side. So his hands remained steady until the sun went down. Joshua defeated Amalek and its army in battle."* - Exodus 17: 9-14 (The Message)

The lesson of this story is twofold. One, in times of challenge and apparent overwhelming odds, when your own strength is at its lowest ebb, raise your hands to God and pray for His power to get you through.

Secondly, when Moses became tired, when his ability to raise his staff in prayer became impossible, his prayers ceased being answered and he needed help. Seek out others who can help you keep your hands raised—others who share your desire to be victorious and ask them to join you in prayer.

Much like Moses, who's raised arms pointing to the heavens represented prayer for safety and victory, constantly pray for your own success and safety on life's journey. Be wary of those times when you become tired and prayer seems like an exercise in futility. It is in those times that you can easily be defeated but it is also in those times when the greatest miracles can happen. On this day, with our tired limbs and battered souls crying out for relief, Mom asked Brownie and Souleman to join her in offering up a prayer that we could continue our quest and asked them to hold her arms up as she did so. This kind of a prayer for strength was answered numerous times as we wearily continued to trudge north.

> *"Be joyful always; pray continually; give thanks in all circumstances, for this is God's will for you in Christ Jesus."*
> – 1 Thessalonians 5:16-17 (NIV)

The events of our lives, just like the events of our hike, are mosaics—works of art comprised of millions of small, yet important, pieces. Our dilemma as humans is that our perspective of that piece of artwork comes from the fact that we view it from up close. We see only the individual pieces and they often do not make sense to us. We see only this present moment in time, our immediate set of circumstances, and we are unable, or unwilling, to see the big picture. But God, who created the mosaic of our lives, stands back from His creation and, in doing so, sees the entire picture—how each piece fits into the entire work and how wonderful and perfect the end result is. Another analogy for God's plan for our lives is that of the championship chess player who has developed the skill to view the entire chessboard at once. He never focuses on the move of just a single piece. From the very first move, he has already planned his last move, carefully moving his pieces accordingly, anticipating what his opponent's next move will be, and ultimately defeats his

## Native American Wisdom

*"Prayer—the daily recognition of the Unseen and the Eternal—is our inevitable duty. We Indian people have traditionally divided mind into two parts—the spiritual mind and the physical mind. The first—the spiritual mind—is concerned only with the essence of things, and it is this we seek to strengthen by spiritual prayer, during which the body is subdued by fasting and hardship. The second, or physical mind, is lower. It is concerned with all personal and selfish matters, like success in hunting or warfare, relief from sickness or the sparing of a beloved one."*

But, in a broader sense, our whole life is prayer because every act of our life is, in a very real sense, a religious act. Our daily devotions are more important to us than food." [9] - Charles Alexander, Ohiyesa, (Dakota

30

erstwhile opponent because each move was part of his plan to reach the desired outcome. He won because he could see the entire match ahead of time.

Because God created the mosaic of our lives, each in its own distinct and unique way, he does not always answer our prayers in the way we desire or expect. Sometimes its feels like He does not answer them at all. However, as the journey of our lives wanders along the path laid out for us, we find that His answers are always right. It is up to us to continually seek the freedom of silence and the sanctuary of solitude required so we can hear His "gentle whisper" in the most unlikely places and experiences. His answers can be found in the commune of nature—in the wind, the rustling of leaves on a brisk fall afternoon, and even in the moist gray cloak of fog that enshrouds a mountaintop.

God has endowed each of us with gifts, abilities and passions. His greatest desire is for us to use them to the best of our ability. His joy is in seeing us joyfully succeed because our success is a reflection of His power, influence and presence in our lives. Before we began our thru-hike, we planned and prepared in order to assure that our adventure, one of a lifetime, would succeed. But, all of that planning and preparation would have been for naught if we had not also prayed for our success. In life, as for a thru-hike, plan, prepare, and work as if it all depends on you, BUT pray as if it all depends on God. Pray endlessly and let your life be an endless prayer.

---

## Devotional: *"Prayer"*

*"Be still and know that I am God."* - Psalm 46:10

When I think about God and his Word, I often have songs come into my head. Sometimes I wonder if they are just a distraction and other times I wonder if it is part of the interaction I should expect in my relationship. Prayer is supposed to be conversational, not just me asking for something or being thankful for something, but a back and forth interaction. So, as I think about being still and listening for God's voice, I hear this song, which has been performed by Chris Tomlin, MercyMe and many others.

*In the secret, in the quiet place*
*In the stillness You are there.*
*In the secret, in the quiet hour I wait,*
*Only for You, 'cause I want to know You more;*

*I want to know You,*
*I want to hear Your voice*
*I want to know You more.*
*I want to touch You,*
*I want to see Your face*
*I want to know You more.*

The song goes on.

Being out on the trail, I would often stop and listen to the quiet. Sometimes this song would come into my head. Is it God—putting the longing into my heart to know Him, to hear His voice, to see His face? I think so. It is one of the things I love so much about being out on the trail—where I can actually hear the quiet and be still. – *Mom*

## Prayer

*"Dear God, I long to hear your voice in the beauty and wonder of your creation—in the still and quiet places."*

# Chapter Three                                        Perseverance

---

*"The most essential factor is persistence - the determination never to allow your energy or enthusiasm to be dampened by the discouragement that must inevitably come."* - James Whitcomb Riley

The technologies and conveniences of our modern age are a wonderful thing. Through computers, cell phones and satellite television we are connected to the entire world. The answers to all our questions, communication with friends and family, and news of the world are only a mouse click, text message, or a TV remote click away.

However, as with any new aspect of progress, there are some surreptitious downsides. The onslaught of technology now provides us with quick answers and quick fixes requiring little, if any, effort to obtain them. We have become accustomed to expecting, and often demanding, that our human needs and problems be addressed, and resolved, in a nanosecond. This high-speed delivery of information has reduced attention spans to the length of a sound bite or a *You Tube®* video—anything requiring more patience, diligence, thought processing time or concentration than that, becomes overwhelming or inconsequential.

So what has happened to so alter our collective understanding of the meaning of progress and achievement? Within the span of the last two-and-a-half decades, how has the demand for instantaneous responses to our every whim, and the expectation of immediate results to our problems, supplanted our fundamental doctrine that real achievement and progress requires hard work, dedication and *perseverance*—the type of perseverance that for over two centuries has characterized the history and strength of our country. Sadly, the value of perseverance seems to be slowly fading from our culture. However, it is perseverance alone that adds an incalculable value to every undertaking, be it a failure or a success. Without it, every effort becomes devoid of passion. The level of a person's perseverance, the ability to keep going and never give up even when every situation screams at them to quit, is the true mark of a person's character. It is a trait that can never be taken away. In the future, what will be the mark of true character if we let perseverance slip away as a worthwhile yardstick?

When a person decides to undertake a long-distance trail, such as the Appalachian Trail, they face a paradigm shift unlike any other and their level of perseverance is challenged daily. They deliberately cut themselves off from the outside world for days, weeks, and even months at a time, with few, if any, technological gizmos at their disposal. With all their worldly possessions on their backs, they are left with but one option in order to succeed—perseverance. It is said, that completing a thru-hike is 20 percent physical and 80 percent mental. There is no easy way to complete a journey of this magnitude but to just keep walking and conquer each new obstacle as it presents itself. There are no technological shortcuts available and the extent of one's self-esteem relies solely on the pursuit of making it from Georgia to Maine, or Maine to Georgia, in one season. If, for whatever reason, one is not able to complete the entire trail, be it as a thru-hike or in sections, it is extremely difficult, to not feel some measure of disappointment, possibly even failure. There is an unparalleled sense of accomplishment and personal satisfaction that overtakes you, as you stand high atop Mt. Katahdin. That defining moment signifies the conclusion of the ultimate quest; an achievement that makes other previous accomplishments seem trivial. The personal growth obtained can positively affect any future endeavor to which one applies himself/herself. Undoubtedly, every future accomplishment will be viewed through the lens of the A.T. experience—a goal that was unattainable without *perseverance*.

Among A.T. hikers, Bill Irwin is quite possibly the epitome of perseverance. In 1990, at the age of fifty with his dog Orient, he became the first person to thru-hike the A.T.—blind. Not only had he fallen victim to a degenerative eye disease at the age of twenty-eight, a disability that stole his independence and sent him spiraling into a state of depression, he also struggled with troubled relationships and was a recovering alcoholic—not exactly the recipe for a successful thru-hike. Yet, after eight and one-half months, an estimated five-thousand falls, and a broken rib, he accomplished a feat that most had deemed impossible. His perseverance reflected not only the strength of his character and will but was an affirmation of his faith in God. His was indeed on a spiritual journey in every respect, a journey that reaped life-long benefits. He has now been working in corporate America for over thirty years, has been a family counselor, has authored a best-selling book about his adventure, and gives motivational presentations all over the world—all this because he tenaciously PERSEVERED. His tenacity is the standard by which many of us gauged our own efforts as we made our way north. There were many days when we were less than satisfied with the level of our own determination when compared with what he faced and overcame. There were even a few times when we attempted to walk the trail with our eyes closed to get a sense of what he had conquered. Alas, we could not travel more than a few feet without either walking off the trail or tripping over something in our way.

Compared to Bill Irwin, our challenges were infinitesimal. Nevertheless, they presented true tests of our own perseverance.

*April 22$^{nd}$*

*"Today we broke the "300-mile barrier," but not without considerable cost to both our physical and mental states. Not long after stepping onto the trail at 7:30 a.m., the rains came, and came and came, so that by lunch we were cold, thoroughly soaked, and more than a bit despondent over our plight. The most disconcerting thing was the condition of our feet. We had just spent almost four weeks getting our feet toughened to the point where they could tolerate most any terrain, but now, after having walked in soaking wet boots for two solid days, our feet had taken on the appearance of flesh-colored prunes and we were right back where we started. We had planned to increase our mileage each day from eight or ten miles to between twelve and sixteen miles. Obviously, those longer miles were not going to be conducive to getting our feet tough while still staving off the potential for blisters.*

*Mom, our intrepid map-reader, perused our trusty topographical map and deduced that we would have an easy day today. According to her assessment, we would be doing mostly "ridge walking"—primarily on the level, even though at some elevations over 4,000 ft. Due to the scale of the map, what was not apparent was that the flat ridges she saw actually consisted of a five to six-mile section of rock climbing. We were constantly scaling near-shear rock faces, climbing precariously steep and narrow rock steps, and proceeding through some very narrow passageways where our packs barely fit through. It was quite a balancing act at times—making our way repeatedly up and over false summits with thirty-five pounds of wet, dead weight strapped to our backs. Even more psychologically debilitating was that, with all the rain, fog and heavy cloud cover blanketing the mountains, we were unable to see anything further away than twenty-five to thirty feet and we knew we were missing some wonderful views.*

*Having despondently made our way over our "ridge walk," we arrived at Jerry Cabin Shelter for lunch just ahead of "Eel," "Old Grandad," and "Melatonin." All we wanted to do right then was get out of the incessant rains that mired our enthusiasm in a constant funk and eat some lunch. As we approached the shelter, we saw that it was inhabited by several hikers, plus all of their wet gear and laundry—most of it hung or draped over every available surface where we might sit. They exhibited an uncharacteristic and unbelievable measure of shelter disrespect. They feigned any modicum of hiker etiquette and made no attempt to clear a place for us to get out of the weather and recuperate. We were forced to stand outside of the shelter in the rain and eat our lunches. Quite disturbed by this turn of events, and floundering even deeper in the emotional and physical morass in which we found ourselves, we set out for Flint Mountain Shelter. Low and behold, when we arrived there we found this shelter also full of hikers holed up due to the rain. Thankfully, with our tempers now reaching a point of detonation, the sun feebly broke through the veil of clouds and mist long enough for us to pitch our tent and make some dinner. It was then that we fervently prayed for sunshine the next day to lift our spirits and dry our boots."* - Windtalker & Mom

*May 20<sup>th</sup>*

*"Today turned out to be, without a doubt, the most physically and emotionally demanding, and exhausting, day we have experienced thus far in our journey. The early-*

*morning weather was wonderfully breezy, sunny and cool. As we left camp we heard the plaintive cry of a coyote off in the woods ahead of us—a cry which I interpreted to be some type of mystical foreshadowing of a remarkable day. We completed a four-mile, 1,500 ft climb, partially up a refreshingly smooth forest road, in record time and stopped at the Audie Murphy Memorial for a break. The site of the memorial is near the spot where this highly decorated World War II veteran, and famed actor, died in a plane crash in 1971. With clear azure skies, tinged by the onset of increasing heat, we made our way to a picnic area near VA 620, Trout Creek, and ate lunch. It was here that we, or should I say I, made what turned out to be a critical mistake. Though there was ample water nearby, we did not check our water supply and did not refill at the creek. For some reason I believed the rest of the day's hike would be relatively easy and that the amount of water we already had would be sufficient. It was a decision that flagrantly went against every bit of good trail-sense I had learned. In fact, so monumental did this oversight become, it easily could have resulted in one or both of our demises. At the very least, it could have suddenly ended our hike.*

*With the temperature in the valley near the creek invitingly cool, and being in a rush to get on the trail as quickly as possible after lunch, I insisted we did not need to refill our water supplies. We would have plenty to last us the rest of the day. We blithely returned to our "walk through spring," reminiscing about our journey thus far and imagining what the rest of the trail held in store. We soon found out! Our pleasant walk in the woods suddenly transformed itself into a horrendous up and down scramble on the stark monolith called "Dragon's Tooth." The temperature had suddenly risen to a summer's day intensity and, as we neared the summit, Mom ran out of water.*

*Now, Mom's metabolism is such that, even as we hiked in the dead of winter, her internal furnace soaked her clothes with sweat and she constantly had to fight off being cold. Whenever temperatures rose to the eighty to ninety-degree mark, this same metabolism required copious amounts of water in order to hold the effects of dehydration at bay. I, on the other hand, was generally oblivious to the onset of* dehydration and rarely drank enough water. My propensity for arriving at camp with a half-full water bladder constantly concerned "Mom," but this day it would be our saving grace.

We talked with numerous hikers who hiked the A.T. multiple times and they were always more than happy to warn us of the difficulties we would encounter. However, in none of those warnings did anyone ever tell us about "Dragon's Tooth" and the danger associated with making our way down its precipitous face. The heat, endless climbing, and rationing of our water began to take its toll on us. We were weak and mentally floundering. We found ourselves verbally snapping at each other for no good reason and had to repeatedly remind each other we were in the same predicament. When we finally arrived at the overlook near the summit, we decided that getting down off this God-forsaken mountain and finding water was more important than another view, so we bypassed the overlook approach trail and started down.

Much to our horror, on top of the physical and mental anguish of not having enough water to renew ourselves, we looked down to see nothing but a bottomless abyss of unforgiving boulders. Even though the presence of the familiar white blazes gave credence to the existence of a trail, so hidden were most of them, we had to arrive at one blaze in order to see the next. Following them required us to scale down numerous headwalls, walk along rock ledges barely as wide as our feet, and then come down the face of large boulders using the metal, ladder-type handles inserted into the rocks for our use. Just the thought of having to go down this section, as tired and as thirsty as we were, brought us to the edge of insanity. Our expectations of a leisurely spring walk had evaporated. In addition to being tired and now firmly entrenched in a dehydration cycle, the weight of our packs often made it difficult to maintain our balance. We were constantly forced away from the surface of the headwalls as we were "free falling," sometimes three to four feet, from one ledge to the next.

It took us nearly three hours to complete this treacherous one-mile section of colossal, geological rubble. We finally arrived at a flat spot where several day-hike trails crossed the A.T. There we took a long rest and attempted to console one another. We shared sips of water from my hydration pack, but *as we did, we heard a sound that struck terror in our souls. It was the wretched and unmistakable gurgling sound of my water bladder getting near empty. My decision not to replenish our water supply at lunch had now come back to haunt us. A choice had to be made—should we continue on to our planned destination for the day or should we take one of the day-hiker trails to the road in search of water? We somewhat reluctantly chose to keep going and immediately realized, much to our disappointment, we had to go up yet another mountain to Rawie's Rest. Despite still being at a rather high elevation, the breeze we had been enjoying had completely disappeared and the heat was now stifling. We gathered what remaining energy we had and shuffled to the top, tiptoeing across a long knife-edge ridge, with what little balance we could muster—which further sapped our determination and will power.*

*As the sun began to give up its sovereignty over the sky, we began our merciful trip to the bottom, sharing sips of what little water we had left. Mom was suffering the most and my consoling words, though meant to be comforting, disguised the fact I was very concerned for her health and safety. Our salvation was an oasis a few miles away, near VA624, where there was supposed to be water and campsites. Knowing this helped to stave off any more doubts we had about surviving the day.*

*As Mom despondently sat near the roadside at VA624 and rested, I set out to locate the water source described in our data book. It took what little remaining constitution I still possessed to make that fruitless excursion and then to return to her and admit that I had been unable to locate any water. We were no better off than before I had left on my quest. We now had to contemplate our options. We could hitchhike into Catawba, Virginia, have dinner at the legendary Homeplace Restaurant, stop by the general store and get water, and then hitch back to the trail. Surprisingly, our state of moroseness and our sapped energy had not adversely affected our ability to think logically. We decided that the time and mileage associated with going to Catawba was equal to the time it would take to hike the next 0.9 mile to a campsite, with a stream nearby, mentioned in our data book. Besides, by the time we went to town, ate, got water and returned to the trail, it would be dark—not a situation we were prepared to deal with considering our present state of mind. Continuing our trek to the campsite became our preferred option, so we pressed forward, all the while hoping our logical decision had not actually been a misguided one—the result of desiccated brain cells.*

*With a single-mindedness of purpose that we hoped would get us to our destination, we climbed up the hill on the north side of the road and into the vast wilderness awaiting us on the other side. We immediately found ourselves on an old forest service road that gently wound downhill through a stand of stately pines. For the first time in hours, we felt good about how the day would end. With twilight fast approaching, we made our way down, down, down, confident water and a place to stay was nearby. As the distant sound of barking coonhounds cascaded through the trees, we arrived at one of the most romantic campsites we could have ever imagined. It looked so peaceful, the cares of the day immediately faded away. Our prayers had been answered and our perseverance rewarded. Nearby, passing under a wooden footbridge, was a refreshing stream so we filled our hydration packs. With bandanas in hand, we also washed away not only the sweaty grime from our bodies but also the soot of melancholy and frustration that had plagued us for most of the day. As the day turned to night, we pitched our tent, enjoyed a delicious dinner under a moonless sky and then crawled into our bags—determined to prevail yet another day."* – Windtalker & Mom

Our perseverance, buttressed by a steady stream of silent prayers, regularly brought us to exactly where we were supposed to be on the trail. This day had been no different. If successfully completing a thru-hike of the Appalachian Trail teaches you nothing else, it teaches you the value and limitless bounds of perseverance and what can be accomplished with it. For those whose lives have a spiritual foundation, a life-long walk of faith is much the same and requires equal, if not more, perseverance.

*"He gives strength to the weary and increases the power of the weak. Even youths grow tired and weary, and young men stumble and fall; but those who hope in the LORD will renew*

*their strength. They will soar on wings like eagles; they will run and not grow weary, they will walk and not be faint." -* Isaiah 40:29-31. (NIV)

We had read all the guidebooks and meticulously planned our journey. To both physically and mentally prepare for our six-month ramble, we went on numerous training hikes. We felt we were ready for anything the trail threw at us. For the first several weeks of our hike, the excitement of what we were undertaking was overwhelming. Rarely did a day go by when, at some point, we did not turn to each other and say, *"Wow! We're hiking the Appalachian Trail!"* It was a new and exciting experience, one that we welcomed, whether the days were hard or easy—the goal of reaching Maine always on our minds.

That euphoric feeling is not unlike the feeling one embraces when becoming a new Christian—it is exciting and enlightening, it makes your spirit soar, and you want to share that excitement with everyone. You immerse yourself in the Bible, God's *life-trail* guidebook, pray for strength and understanding, and head out onto your new "path" with a compelling sense of resolve. Nothing will stand in your way and your desire to succeed in your spiritual pilgrimage knows no limits. You are steadfast in your beliefs, but rest assured, your level of excitement, knowledge, and the understanding you have of your new life, will constantly be tested.

As time wore on, hiking those 2,175 miles provided many days that were just HARD WORK! All of the training and preparation seemed mere footnotes to the seemingly unending obstacles that the trail put in our way. We were often tired and our bodies were in constant pain. Because of this, our level of excitement sometimes waned a bit and we began to experience random moments of doubt about our ability to continue. To finish each day and to finish the trail, we needed perseverance. As Christians, we are encouraged to spiritually persevere as well. A walk of faith is often no different than hiking the A.T. and, just like those days of self-doubt on the trail, only perseverance keeps you moving forward on your journey of faith.

*"Walking freely is not about walking without struggle; it is about walking without our struggles controlling us. As we are transformed into the image of Christ and continue to be obedient, I think certain things become—dare I say—easier. Our gnawing fears and addictions and our wayward tendencies aren't so overpowering. I think we develop a*

*greater capacity to trust God each time we take a step out in faith and overcome our urges to do otherwise. We may walk with a limp, but we walk nonetheless."* [10] - Kelly Minter

There will be times when your faith is challenged, when the world around you seems to run counter to everything you currently believe. You begin to wonder if your level of faith is sufficient to overcome all the obstacles that litter your spiritual path. Not only maintaining your own faith, but also sharing your faith with others, may seem implausible. When we began our journey, we firmly believed that with all of our planning and training we would have no trouble completing our odyssey. It was not long before the gravity of just how challenging the A.T. was had us wondering if we had prepared at all. It became obvious that just being excited about our adventure would not be adequate to have us prevail. All our preparation and planning had not been in vain, however. Though the demands of the trail exceeded what physical preparation we initially brought to the table, what our preparation and planning did do was endow us with the mental and emotional capacity to accept and adapt to the challenges we faced. Likewise, it can become discouraging if one goes headlong into a walk of faith believing that one's newly found faith alone will be sufficient. It is essential to develop realistic expectations based on your current level of understanding, spiritual maturity, and the tools (wisdom) you have at the moment. Continue to study and learn, for with each new piece of wisdom and understanding you gain, you will become better prepared to accept and adapt to the unexpected circumstances that life brings your way.

The driving force that kept us moving forward on the trail was the vision in the back of our minds of triumphantly standing atop Mt. Katahdin—our trekking poles stretched toward the heavens in celebration and our souls reaching a level of satisfaction we had never felt before. We overcame, we grew, and most importantly, we kept our eyes on the prize so we could finish well!

### Native American Wisdom

*"When you begin a great work you can't expect to finish it all at once; therefore do you and your brothers press on and let nothing discourage you until you have entirely finished what you have begun.*

*Now Brother, as for me, I assure you I will press on, and the contrary winds may blow strong in my face, yet I will go forward and never turn back and continue to press forward until I have finished, and I would have you do the same..."* [11] - Teedyuscung (Delaware)

*"Brothers, I do not consider myself yet to have taken hold of it. But one thing I do: Forgetting what is behind and straining toward what is ahead, I press on toward the goal to win the prize for which God has called me heavenward in Christ Jesus."* - Philippians 3:13-14 (NIV)

Perseverance is not a trait that one is born with. It can be taught, but ultimately it comes down to a choice. Parents can display examples of perseverance for their children, but their children must recognize its intrinsic value and choose perseverance as a life-style for themselves. Even as adults, we can be inspired by the perseverance of others, such as Bill Irwin or Lee Barry, who completed his final thru-hike in 2004 at the age of 81. Still, it is a conscious choice for us to translate that inspiration into action.

Many of the people on the trail, despite their physical fitness, chose to discontinue their hike—not because they were injured, but because they were bored, frustrated or dissatisfied. Quite possibly, they had not seen perseverance demonstrated to them, did not recognize it when they did see it, or they simply chose not to use it because of the hard work it requires; if they only understood how satisfying it is to persevere and succeed. Yet there were those like twelve-year-old Brandon of "The Wanderers." He displayed remarkable perseverance for someone so young by completing a northbound trek with his dad and sister despite having his broken arm in a cast from a fall on Sugarloaf Mountain in Maine. In contrast to his counterparts, who left the trail, he kept his eye on the prize and knew that perseverance would offer incredible rewards.

Perhaps one of the most dramatic displays of perseverance, this side of Bill Irwin, was the group of thru-hikers who succeeded in completing their journey in 2003. This was a year plagued with seven straight weeks of rain, where these brave souls never experienced a day in dry clothes or in a dry tent. It was said that some had their boots literally rot off their feet. The constant misery of never being dry should have been enough to drive even the heartiest hiker from the trail. However, they trudged on, displaying a level of fortitude and determination that is as remarkable as it is inspiring.

The key to persevering and succeeding in a Christian walk is to also keep your eye on the prize and finish well. If we do this, God will provide the strength we need to succeed.

*"Do you see what this means—all these pioneers who blazed the way, all these veterans cheering us on? It means we'd better get on with it. Strip down, start running—and never quit! No extra spiritual fat, no parasitic sins. Keep your eyes on Jesus, who both began and finished this race we're in. Study how he did it. Because he never lost sight of where he was headed—that exhilarating finish in and with God—he could put up with anything along the way: Cross, shame, whatever. And now he's there, in the place of honor, right alongside God. When you find yourselves flagging in your faith, go over that story again, item by item, that long litany of hostility he plowed through. That will shoot adrenaline into your souls!"* – Hebrews 12:1-3 (The Message)

For us, as we are sure it was for virtually every thru-hiker, the days requiring perseverance easily outweighed the days that did not. However, we knew those difficult days would eventually pass. Those difficult days challenged everything we believed about ourselves, but also brought with them the most personal gain. When the day ended and we had reached our destination, we celebrated our success and felt a profound sense of peace. There was also a visceral understanding that our character had developed to a new level.

*August 23$^{rd}$: Destination: AMC Nauman Tent Site (Mizpah Shelter area)*

*"As we crawled from our tent this morning, ate breakfast and re-packed our backpacks, the relentless and near-debilitating aches and pains, vestiges of yesterday's 14.5-mile trek, impeded our every move. The constant groans of agony emanating from every muscle and tendon were going to make today's ten miles of steep and dangerous ascents and descents all that more formidable. What lay ahead of us was some of the most difficult terrain on the trail.*

*After re-stocking with V&A, we left Crawford Notch and began the grueling 2,630 ft climb up to the summit of Mt. Webster (3,910 ft); taking us past Webster Cliffs (3,330 ft) where we planned to stop for lunch and revel in the monumental views. One particular section up to the summit of Mt. Webster required some intensive hand-over-hand climbing up a near vertical precipice whose unstable surface of mud, roots, and loose rocks threatened to give way with each step. It was all we could do to keep our fear of plummeting to the valley's floor in check. We also had to battle very windy conditions gusting down from the summit above.*

*As if our climb was not perilous enough, once we reached the summit, we now had to descend long stretches of practically vertical rocks faces in winds between twenty-five to forty miles per hour. These conditions, along with our growing fatigue, made travel even more tenuous. We found ourselves proceeding down these rock faces safely sitting on our butts most of the way. We became quite despondent when, as we gingerly slid down one particularly huge boulder face, two teenage boys flew by us walking straight down the face of the same boulder, as if they were on flat ground—not even breaking stride. Then, as if that sight was not enough to curb our enthusiasm even further, we had to scale Mt. Jackson (4,052 ft) with even more wind and still more hand-over-hand climbing.*

*As mid-afternoon approached, our hiking speed had dropped to 1.0 mph, thus increasing our frustration. We knew from the very beginning of our journey that we would be forced to slow our pace in The White Mountains because of their rugged and treacherous nature. We simply were not prepared to be slowed quite this much. We began to be concerned as to whether or not we would be able to do the twelve miles up and over Mt. Washington in a single day. Since Mt. Washington has the storied reputation for the worst and most unpredictable weather in the U.S., one does not want to get caught on it if the weather turns ugly—a situation that can develop very quickly. We had to force that concern from our minds because there is no place to stay overnight at the top of Mt. Washington. We would simply have to make it.*

*As the sun began to make a hasty retreat into the valley below, we reached the AMC Mizpah Hut/Nauman Tentsite. We set up our tent, ate, got some critical information from the caretaker, and called it a day. It had been a day marked by seemingly overwhelming obstacles that tested our will, physical endurance, and ability to shake off the haunting ghosts of doubt and insecurity that threatened to cloud our judgment, and undermine our perseverance. As we looked back on the day, our bodies still screaming for relief from the torture they had been put through, we realized that it had been another life-changing day—a day when our mantra of quitting not being an option had not only survived but had prevailed. "* – Windtalker & Mom

On a walk of faith, learning to accept every obstacle and challenge in life is an opportunity to grow spiritually. Despite how difficult situations may seem, knowing that God is control and that his plan for every life is designed to strengthen character, the result is a deepening of faith and an ever-increasing belief in one's ability to persevere. It is through those trying times that God's greatest desire, the desire to have an intimate relationship with you, manifests itself.

*"Not only so, but we also rejoice in our sufferings, because we know that suffering produces perseverance; perseverance, character; and character, hope. And hope does not disappoint us, because God has poured out his love into our hearts by the Holy Spirit, whom he has given us."* - Romans 5:3-5 (NIV)

On our six-month pilgrimage, it was easier for us to persevere because we had a support team that provided both encouragement and assistance. We benefitted from having Mom's parents along for the journey in their RV, meeting us at road crossings with our supplies. There were our fellow, "like-minded," hikers who challenged and encouraged us every step of the way. They offered help and compassion based on their own experiences. Then, there were the trail angels who provided us with food and drinks at the most unexpected, yet opportune moments. All of these people shared a common vision and mission—the success of our struggle to reach Mt. Katahdin. They understood what we were enduring each day and when we were tired, sore, hungry, and sweaty they were our cheerleaders, bolstering our spirits and reminding us of why we must continue.

In a Christian walk, there are also times of trial, times when you are spiritually tired, sore, hungry and sweaty. In those times it is good to be surrounded by your own "spiritual trail angels"—those who share in your love of Christ. Be it a small group or life group, a prayer group, a bible study group, or a specific ministry that can benefit from your God-given gifts and talents, it will be easier to persevere with them at your side every step of the way.

*"Consider it a sheer gift, friends, when tests and challenges come at you from all sides. You know that under pressure, your faith-life is forced into the open and shows its true colors. So don't try to get out of anything prematurely. Let it do its work so you become mature and well-developed, not deficient in any way."* - James 1:2-4 (The Message)

Walk on!

---

## Devotional: *"Perseverance"*

*"Consider it pure joy, my brothers, whenever you face trials of many kinds, because you know that the testing of your faith develops perseverance."* - James 1:2-3

I recall a point in my life when my Dad and I were talking about an increase in teen and young adult suicides and he said, *"I hope that I've raised you kids to know that the bad days will always pass."* It was an encouragement about life and a reminder to me that I've often thought of since then. Later, there was a rough patch in my life at work so I printed out a dozen Bible passages on patience, perseverance, and long-suffering. I needed a daily reminder and encouragement that I should just hang on.

In Paul's letter to the Romans, he advised that suffering produces perseverance; perseverance, character; and character, hope. However, he starts out his letter to the Christians in Rome with encouragement, telling them how he was praying for them and how he wanted to be able to share gifts with them so that they could be mutually encouraged. In the King James Version of the above passage, James also starts out with an encouragement to "count it all joy!" Yes, he said ALL; good and bad! In fact, he also later says in verse 12:

*"Blessed is the man who perseveres under trial, because when he has stood the test, he will receive the crown of life that God has promised to those who love him."*

So, we persevered on the trail, through the rain, through the pain, all the way to win the prize—Mt. Katahdin, in Maine. And yes, all the encouragement from everyone around us helped! So what do we get

when we persevere in a life of faith? Character, hope, and eternal life. Hiking the trail was such a short opportunity for developing perseverance and a short opportunity to encourage each other to persevere! Let us continue to encourage each other to persevere in life!
– *Mom*

## Prayer

*"God give me the strength, courage, and reckless abandon to live each moment of each day to the very end of my life with joy... pursuing you and pursuing the dreams you have hidden in my heart. Help me encourage everyone around me."*

# Chapter Four

# Family and Community

> *"Treasure your relationships, not your possessions."* -
> Anthony J. D'Angelo

Every year since 1986, the town of Damascus, Virginia, billed as *The Friendliest Town on the Appalachian Trail*, has held an annual "Appalachian Trail Days Festival." This multi-day event, sort of a hiker version of Woodstock, brings together the town's people and thru-hikers, past, present and future, to enjoy music, seminars, peruse the latest hiking equipment and to participate in the always colorful and outrageously funny hiker parade down the town's main street. More important than the scheduled events that make up Trail Days is that it is a time for thru-hikers to renew old friendships, create new ones and swap tales of their experiences on the A.T. Each year Trail Days revolves around a theme and in 2008, the theme was *"People Are the Trail."* A more apt slogan could not have been chosen, for without the people on and along the trail, the memories of making such a journey would be greatly diminished. Thru-hikers, and the people who support them along the way, consider each other part of a special family—custodians of a legacy of strength, perseverance, courage, compassion and triumph. All of our lives are forever etched by the relationships made during our journey.

> *"For better or for worse, families shape us. We are all God's family, and like our own families, God's family also changes and influences us. However, we also shape the family."* [12] -
> Paul Abbott, Pastor, Cedarbrook Community Church

For us, two introverts, becoming part of a trail community or "trail family" was not in the forefront of our minds when we discussed the many things that our A.T. adventure would incorporate. Our concept of a memorable journey included grandiose vistas, fresh air, craggy mountains, crystal-clear lakes and encounters with wild animals we had only seen in photos. Socializing with other hikers and cultivating relationships was not a planned activity. The reason for this was that, unlike extroverts who rely on social interaction as the means to keep themselves happy and healthy, our emotional batteries are recharged by solitude; our personal satisfaction is derived from hours of quiet reflection. This is not to say we are recluses or that we do not enjoy social interaction, it just is not what makes us tick. Being on the trail was intended to be a prolonged period of solitude and reflection away from the crowds, traffic and tumult of our urban lives near Washington, DC—not an opportunity to develop relationships.

However, the extent to which we could adhere to our introverted tendencies was immediately under siege by the mere fact that there was such a huge number of thru-hikers heading north with us. Short of being extremely rude, it was virtually impossible not to interact with them in some way each day. We all began this miraculous journey as strangers, each one striving to make sense of the personal reason that brought each of us to this point in our lives. The enthusiasm for the adventure we shared was contagious and the adventure became the common ground on which relationships quickly grew. In a spiritual sense, we were all foreigners—struggling to get the lay of the land, to

> ### Native American Wisdom
>
> *"In Western culture, emphasis is placed on the nuclear family—dad, mom, brothers, sisters and grandparents. In Native culture, the extended family is given great importance; father, mother, brothers, sisters, grandparents, uncles, aunts, cousins, nieces, nephews and in-laws. In traditional Lakota/Sioux culture, each individual enjoyed the security of belonging to the "tiyospaye," or "extended family." Though it is no longer what it once was, it is still a highly valued and vital reality in Lakota social structure."* [13] – Richard Twiss, Taoyate Obnajin (Lakota/Sioux)

understand the language, to fit into the culture without losing our own sense of identity and to become productive members of the community. We soon learned that being a part of the trail family of thru-hikers was not only enjoyable, providing an added dimension to the adventure, but was essential in guaranteeing safety and success. Our communally shared dream of conquering the Appalachian Trail and standing triumphantly atop Mt. Katahdin was the glue that bound all of us together. Our mutual mission and vision overshadowed our differences in age, background, personality, ethnicity, education, financial status and marital status. We were all on the same path, following the same guidebook and with the same goal in mind. We quickly became a *fellowship of wanderers* and that fellowship bridged the superficial gaps that otherwise might have prevented us from possibly ever meeting. The goal of walking all the way to Maine became the common thread that brought us to encourage and support each other on those days when it was near impossible to continue by only one's own willpower. We happily discovered that *People are the Trail* was more than a gratuitous catchphrase. As it turned out over the course of our six months on the trail, we spent time with over one-hundred-fifty different hikers with unlikely, yet unforgettable trail names such as "Brownie," "Old Drum," "E-Rock," "Lichen," "Carbomb," Trickster," "Burner" and "Bama." Many other hikers made brief cameo appearances and each influenced our perspective on relationships and life itself. We are still in contact with many of them and are humbled to be called their friends.

Being part of a trail family is based on the sharing of everyday experiences, oftentimes at the exact same time. Each day you share the trials and tribulations. You hike in rain. You hike in sleet. You hike in the cold and you hike in the heat. You share the gorgeous lakes and streams. You see the grand sunsets and full moons together. You sleep shoulder-to-shoulder in crowded, mouse-infested shelters, as sleet pounds on the shelter's metal roof. You experience the same wondrous views from the mountaintops above tree line. You also point out to each other the cairn five feet ahead on a mountaintop trail when the fog is so thick you can barely see your feet. This bond with your fellow travelers influences your decision to stop and linger in that fog at the summit of places like Mt. Moosilauke, until your family arrives so you can take photos of each other and share the joy of being above treeline for the first time. This astonishing journey is your life and you are all doing life together. We often lamented the fate of the southbound A.T. thru-hikers who, because of the dearth of hikers heading north to south, had fewer opportunities to share the joys and frustrations of their journey. They also missed developing the closeness of trail family that we enjoyed and treasured by hiking north.

This sharing of trail life binds thru-hikers' souls and personalities together in a way unique to the A.T. Another life experience that can match the level of excitement, understanding, caring and camaraderie that being a part of a trail family affords is that of a journey of faith. In a spiritual or Christian environment, relationships are often developed in a church setting, in small groups, care groups, life groups, or whatever term a given church may give them. The people in these groups comprise your Christian family and it is here that you *do life together*.

As do A.T. thru-hikers, the people in a Christian family also share a common goal, walk a common path, and follow the same "guide book." Because of their journey of faith, members of these groups share trials and tribulations similar to those experienced on the trail. Just as a trail family suffers loss (e.g., a fellow hiker leaving the trail due to injury), our own small group, as an example, has suffered together through miscarriages and family deaths. Christian families have ups and downs (hiking in the cold and in the heat), lives are blessed with moments of wonder (seeing the grand sunsets and full moons together) and episodes of triumph (safely negotiating through Mahoosuc Notch or standing atop Mt. Katahdin).

The purpose for your Christian family's spiritual journey and its eternal destination also binds people together; differences in age, gender, financial position, marital status, education or social status are of no consequence. They come together to congratulate, consol, educate, encourage, challenge, share, hold accountable, and most importantly, share the blessings, forgiveness and grace that their shared faith affords them. The goal of faith families is the same as that of the thru-hiking trail families—that everyone will successfully reach the mountaintop that marks the end of their journey and making that journey has made them better people, as well as having been a benefit to others.

> *"Let us not give up meeting together, as some are in the habit of doing, but let us encourage one another—and all the more as you see the Day approaching."* - Hebrews 10:25 (NIV)

> *"Let us not become weary in doing good, for at the proper time we will reap a harvest if we do not give up. Therefore, as we have opportunity, let us do good to all people, especially to those who belong to the family of believers."* - Galatians 6:9-10 (NIV)

Along with all the positive memorable experiences and accomplishments from our lives, each one of us also carries emotional and psychological baggage—remnants of life's less-than-stellar experiences. Some of those unfortunate experiences take a toll on our joy and impacts our view of life. Like carrying a backpack laden with thirty-some pounds of gear, emotional weight slows us down, wears us out and influences what direction we decide to take. Moreover, just like that backpack, you eventually get accustomed to life's baggage being there, but there is no escaping the affect extra baggage has on you. Ironically, that very same baggage is an essential part of your journey. The gear and food you carry on the trail is heavy and can sometimes be a source of recurring pain and aggravation. However, without what is in that pack, you could not move on to your destination. The weight is a constant reminder that you are alive and still pursuing your goal.

We labor each day under the weight of our packs (baggage) and the longer we are on the trail (live) the more we sweat and the more we smell. That smell is analogous to our negative attitudes, things we have done wrong, and how we may have offended or hurt other people. When thru-hikers arrive in a town after five to seven days on the trail, quite frankly they STINK. Even if they are not carrying packs or loping along with trekking poles, the smell is an obvious indication that they have been traveling for a long time. And yet, even with the funky aroma of a week's worth of perspiration wafting from every pore, there are those along the trail and in town who see past that aroma and welcome them with open arms. These compassionate people, trail angels as they are affectionately referred to, are also part of your trail family. As part of that family, they see it as their ardent responsibility to care for you—with housing, food, encouragement, a much-needed shower and a soft, warm bed.

Though few trail angels verbally profess a life of faith, through devoting their lives to helping and encouraging thru-hikers on their twenty-one hundred and seventy-five mile quest for renown, they unquestionably exemplify the very heart of the Christian ethic. Nowhere will one find such unselfish devotion to the well-being of his fellow man and such unbridled compassion for perfect strangers. Each time we received the benefits of their love for us, we could not help but feel that, even if they were not aware of it, their actions exemplified the type of life God calls us all to lead. For many hikers, the help of these trail angels was merely a wonderful gift provided when they least expected it and needed it the most. For us, the actions of trail angels were unquestionably spiritual and their impact on each person they touched, eternal and inspirational. Their approach to meeting the needs of their fellow man on the trail mirrors how each of us should meet the needs of our fellow travelers on the *trail of life*. In the Book of Mathew, Jesus uses a parable to explain to His disciples how man's helping the needy is actually displaying love and compassion for God—the very actions we saw time and time again during our six-month sojourn.

*"I was hungry and you fed me,*
*I was thirsty and you gave me a drink,*
*I was homeless and you gave me a room,*
*I was shivering and you gave me clothes,*
*I was sick and you stopped to visit,*
*I was in prison and you came to me.'*

*...'Master, what are you talking about? When did we ever see you hungry and feed you, thirsty and give you a drink? And when did we ever see you sick or in prison and come to you?'*

*Then the King will say, 'I'm telling the solemn truth: Whenever you did one of these things to someone overlooked or ignored, that was me—you did it to me."* - Mathew 25: 35-40 (The Message)

We had the opportunity to live out this calling ourselves on more than one occasion. While making a long, steep ascent of one of the many mountains in Georgia that challenged every ounce of fortitude we possessed, we came upon "Granny Franny." We watched her staggering up the trail, greatly off balance, with her pack mercilessly flopping around on her back. As she stopped to sit on a log to take a break from her ordeal, we asked if she was all right. Few thru-hikers will admit they are having trouble, especially this early in their journey, but despite her assurances to us that she was fine, we offered to adjust her pack and ease her burden a bit. The last we saw of her, she was coming up the trail behind us with a quite a bit less effort after we helped adjust her pack.

Our second chance came at Hogback Ridge Shelter, in Tennessee, when we stopped for an early dinner before continuing on to Low Gap for the evening. When we arrived at the shelter, "Bluebird" and "Melatonin" were already there and had decided that they would be staying for the night. "Bluebird" informed us that because she had slowed her pace several days earlier in order to minimize the damage to her feet and legs, she was now dangerously low on food. With her next supply stop still several days away, she was certain she would not have enough to make it. We both rustled through our packs and came up with several meals for her. We always brought extra food, should we be held up by bad weather and need to hunker down for a day or two. We were also a bit ahead of schedule so we would get to our next supply stop sooner than expected. It felt good to be able to help a fellow hiker, and as a side benefit, we now had less weight to carry.

*March 31^st^:*

*"It was the final day of March and our night on Tray Mountain at 3,580 feet had been truly outstanding! A brilliant slice of moon pierced the clear, pitch-black sky, unfettered by clouds or mist. We could easily see the twinkling lights of the homes in the gaps many miles below us—earthly reflections of the millions of stars that hung overhead. We sat outside our tent for awhile, gazing into that valley, trying to imagine what twists and turns of life were taking place in those homes. And as we voyeuristically passed the time, we realized how different our lives were now—emotionally and psychologically as far from what they had been only a few days ago as we were physically from those homes in the gap.*

*Not long after crawling into our tent, the peaceful respite in which we had just been reveling was suddenly and unabashedly torn from us! The wind came up from the valley, building to an ear-piercing crescendo, until it sounded like a 747 passing just a few feet overhead. It continued over our tent, buffeting the rain fly on our tent like a sail in a hurricane, and then plummeted into the gap on the other side. Wave after wave of nature's raw and glorious power washed over us and it was frighteningly wonderful. It was a lullaby that lulled us into a deep and restful sleep.*

*The next morning, as it had on so many other mornings, clouds settled in on top of the mountain, blocking the sun and covering everything in sight with a sloppy layer of dew. We got a late start, 7:45 a.m., and soon realized we were experiencing quite a bit more foot pain than usual. The morning's long climbs and accompanying long descents only exacerbated the discomfort but there was no way it was going to stop us. The sun finally broke through, beginning as mere "sun dogs" piercing the roof of clouds, offering us hope that the day was going to be yet another memorable one. As the sun finally exploded into full view, it evaporated the mist from the surrounding hillsides and it began to get quite warm. We stopped at Deep Gap at 3,550 feet for lunch and a much-needed "boots-off/pack-off" break before starting the*

*1,175 feet, 2.2-mile descent to our day's destination. As we neared the final gap, walking through a tunnel of rhododendron, gasping for breath, and repeatedly wiping sweat from our foreheads, there it was—"trail magic!" "Hike-Ku" had left cans of Mountain Dew in a stream near the trail, along with packages of my all-time favorite, Nutty-Buddy Bars®. He had also left a hand-written sign in the middle of the trail letting everyone know where these delights were located. This introduction to the unexpected and glorious experience that is "trail magic" was only a portent of what was to come.*

*We arrived at Dick's Creek Gap late in the afternoon and V&A gave us a ride to the Blue Berry Patch Hostel—our sanctuary for the night. But first, there was more "magic!" V&A brought us fried chicken, coleslaw, biscuits, peach cobbler, and orange sodas for dinner. We were so starved that just the smells emanating from those red and white bags, with Colonel Sanders' cartoon portrait printed on the front, had us drooling before we ever got out of the car at the hostel.*

*For years, Gary and Lennie Poteat have been welcoming hikers into their quaint hostel, a large converted garage next to their home. Being a thru-hiker himself, Gary is very familiar with life on the trail. The hostel, complete with several picnic tables placed end to end, comfortable bunks, a hot plate and a refrigerator full of cold sodas, was like heaven on earth to us—perhaps that is what is it was designed to convey. Being devout Christians, Gary and Lennie have never shied away from proclaiming their faith and every thru-hiker guide notes that fact. Operating this hostel is a ministry for them and they are proud of it. Their love and care for hikers is a visible manifestation of their faith.*

*Out back, overlooking the large garden where they harvest their own vegetables and blueberries, guarded by a small herd of pet donkeys, was the shower house. Being able to wash away the stink and grime we had accumulated over the last few days was a luxurious treat. We felt like human beings again—and we again smelled like it too. While we showered, Lennie did our laundry so it was finished when we returned. We polished off our KFC® dinner with the help of*

*"Dave," our hostel mate for the evening, and hit the sack. We were anxious to partake of one of their acclaimed breakfasts the next morning.*

*Mom battled leg cramps most of the night but awoke, as I did, refreshed and ready for breakfast. We shuffled into Gary and Lennie's comfortable sunroom, sat down at a huge oak table near their antique wood cook stove, and joined both of them in prayer. Communal praying was something we had been sorely missing while on the trail, though we did silently pray each day that we would make it safely to Katahdin. Then it was time to dig in. Living primarily off the land, the Poteats serve natural, home-cooked treats such as eggs, pancakes with their homemade blueberry syrup, biscuits, sausage, orange juice, and coffee.*

*In everything they said and did, it was obvious to us they were devoted not only to God and hikers, but to each other as well. We learned a great deal simply by watching and listening to them. Because of their love for us, our faith in not only people but also in God, was strengthened. It seemed that more and more couples were being unexpectedly put in our path as inspiration for our relationship and our lives."* - Windtalker & Mom

*July 26th:*

*"It was almost the end of July and for the last several days we had been hearing from other hikers about a couple who had positioned themselves on the trail at Benedict Pond. There they were providing hot meals like eggs, bacon, hamburgers, hotdogs and cold drinks. We anxiously looked forward to meeting them and partaking of the delicacies they were offering to all the starving wanderers that passed their way. Unfortunately, because we left our campsite so early in the morning, when we arrived where they stationed themselves, they had yet to arrive. However, sitting in a small clearing near the lake, sat their grill, four chairs and a cooler. There was also a note from "Mr. & Mrs. Tunes" apologizing for missing us and instructing us to help ourselves to the drinks and food hidden under the lid of the grill. It was only 7:30 a.m., a bit early for soda, but Mom and I split a Sierra Mist®. The compassion of these trail angels,*

*members of our ever-growing trail family, inspired us to leave a roll of toilet paper behind for some other needy hiker. It was our way of "passing forward" the generosity they showed us."* - Windtalker & Mom

Having a "family of faith" is in truth no different from having trail angels along the trail. This family also sees past your smell, the results of the negative baggage you are burdened with, and also welcomes you in. In those times when that baggage becomes more than you think you can carry alone, your faith and your family can help lighten the load. Many of them have been where you may be in your life and their compassion and understanding, based on their own experience and solid Christian beliefs, can carry you through. They become your own *spiritual trail angels* providing compassion, understanding, encouragement and a safe, warm place to rest for a while.

> Native American Wisdom
>
> *"Oh the comfort, the inexpressible comfort of feeling safe with a person, having neither to weigh thought nor measure words, but pouring them all right out, just as they are, chaff and grain together, certain that a faithful hand will take and sift them, keep what is worth keeping, and with a breath of kindness, blow the rest away."* [14]
> Anonymous (Shoshone)

Nestled in the heart of the Lehigh Valley in Pennsylvania, two miles from the Lehigh River, is the quaint little town of Palmerton. Well known by hikers for the nearby precipitous and nerve-wracking climb out of Lehigh Gap to the moonscape rubble above, a summit stripped bare by years of uncontrolled zinc mining, the town is equally well-known for its unique hostel. Operated by the town in the basement of its old jail, the Palmerton experience is the quintessential example of the type of hospitality offered to many a weary and smelly thru-hiker. The town's people exemplify what it means to offer unconditional compassion and understanding to perfect strangers—simply because they are in desperate need of a shower and a place to lay their heads. They do not care who you are, where you come from, whether you are a nice person or not, or that you smell incredibly bad. As you walk through the front door, you are immediately accepted as part of their trail family and they do what a family does. Their actions leave a lasting impression on every hiker who stops in to benefit from their benevolence.

*July 5th:*

"*Today was quite a day—not very long, but extremely memorable in so many ways. We woke up to a drenching rain that forced its way through the rich canopy of foliage above us, soaking everything in sight, and turning our campsite into a quagmire. It was not an auspicious beginning to our long descent into Lehigh Gap. We heard the morning rain would eventually end but there were also predictions of additional late afternoon thunderstorms, a meteorological state of affairs that we had become accustomed to dealing with as of late. Not wanting to pack up a wet tent in the rain, we modified our plans for the day somewhat. The heaviest rains let up at 10:30 a.m., so we waited until then, packed up and headed out—though we were still forced to hike in showers on and off most of the morning. It was just after a brief brunch, still uncertain of how our afternoon would play out, when we ran into "Ridgerunner Roger." He strongly advised against us attempting the ascent out of Lehigh Gap in the afternoon with thunderstorms in the weather forecast.*

*'That ascent is EXTREMELY steep and difficult and once you get to the top you still have miles of totally exposed mountaintop to walk across, with absolutely no place to hide from lightning,' he warned us.*

*Upon hearing this, we made our decision to rendezvous with V&A outside of Palmerton and hold up there for the night till the weather stabilized. The sun finally did come out but not until we were heading down the final steep descent to Lehigh Gap. We treated ourselves to large handfuls of blueberries along the way and washed them down with ice-cold Cokes® Ridgerunner Roger had left in one of the springs we passed. Wanting to experience as many of the "historic elements" of the trail as possible, we decided we would stay the night at the old Palmerton jail. There we could partake of the essentials of a hot shower and a real bed, free from any more rain. Excited about this brief excursion to one of the icons of the A.T., we had V&A drive us into town to experience for ourselves if all the wonderful stories we had heard were indeed true.*

*When the town built its new police station and jail, the old one was converted into town offices and a community activities center. The townspeople decided to turn the basement, which previously housed the jail, into a hostel for hikers. It also serves as a meeting place for local scout troops. The facility is large, with showers, bunk beds, tables, benches, towels, a hiker box, and a furnace room where you can hang your wet gear to dry (we would certainly take advantage of this last amenity since most of our clothes were soaked). And, if you still had the energy after a day's worth of hiking, there is an indoor basketball court just off the shower room. When we first arrived and signed in, we were presented with "goodie bags" prepared by one of the local Girl Scout troops. It contained toothpaste, a toothbrush, a small roll of toilet paper, and a card letting us know who put together our "goodie bags." All of this was provided absolutely "free of charge" and was indicative of how we were treated by everyone we met in town—from the waitress at Bert's Steakhouse, where we had dinner, to the folks at the IGA supermarket where we went to pick up a few things. Everyone was extremely friendly. They waved at us and took a genuine interest in what we were attempting to accomplish. They were sincerely glad to see us, which was comforting, and their warm hospitality was so different from what we were accustomed to at home. We began to utterly detest the unfriendly atmosphere of D.C. suburbia and looked forward to being away from it for as long as possible. We also wished we could have been there the day before because we were certain that this was the type of town that put on a splendid Fourth of July celebration—complete with a parade and fireworks.*

*After our home-style dinner, we sat in the cool evening air on the front steps of the jail waiting for the evening cleaning crew to arrive and unlock the front door so we could get back in. As we sat watching the pleasingly sporadic parade of traffic on Main Street, where pedestrians actually received the right of way, a gentleman strolled up and stopped right in front of us.*

*'Hi, my name's Kevin. Do you folks need a ride back to the trail in the morning?'*

*'Thanks! That would be great. My name is Windtalker and this is Mom.*

*Since most people in Palmerton do not generally walk around town in Crocs®, the fact we had ours on was Kevin's first clue we were from out of town—and the far-away look in our eyes confirmed we were thru-hikers. Kevin, a.k.a. "Billygoat," and his wife, "Granola," are trail angels and regularly provide shuttles and trail magic to hikers. We confirmed what time he would pick us up in the morning and headed inside to go to sleep—sleep that was suddenly interrupted mid-course by a colossal thunderstorm that dropped untold inches of rain on the area. At that moment, we were very glad we had heeded "Ridgerunner Roger's" sage advice and had stayed in town. Had we not, our fate up on the ridgeline would have been questionable at best and disastrous at worst. Besides, if we had not come into Palmerton we would have missed the chance to be cared for and encouraged by members of our trail family."* - Windtalker & Mom

Considering how vast and uninhabited most of the Appalachian Trail is, it was always a source of amazement to us as to how many people we actually met on the trail. Some we hiked with or spent the evening with in a shelter. Some we saw just in passing as they made their way down the trail in the opposite direction. Still others were the townspeople or the operators of the many hostels and outfitters along the way. The further we traveled the more we looked forward to the chances to meet these people, getting to know them, and sharing a bit of life with them—and they with us. Spiritually speaking, much like Abraham in the Book of Genesis, we just never knew when we might be "entertaining angels," and little did they know how much of an encouragement their brief interlude with us might be.

*May 21st:*

*"Another beautiful May day. We had to wonder when it was going to end, though we prayed that it would not be soon. We stopped for a lunch of chicken and dumplings with V&A in their RV, which was parked at a road crossing at the base of one of the most famous and most photographed overlooks*

*on the A.T.—McAfee Knob. It was rare that a hiker did not gingerly venture to the overlook's mammoth ledge, sit down with legs hanging out in mid-air, and have his/her picture taken. As we exited the RV, with our stomachs way too full, we feared, to make the long climb to the summit, we stopped to talk with ridge runner Bob Stimson who was leaving to check up on a large group of hikers on their way up. In accordance with his job description, he was planning to make sure they followed "Leave No Trace" practices, leaving no noticeable impact of their presence on the trail. We had decided on a very short day since we had not yet recovered from our run-in with Dragon's Tooth yesterday—our goal being the Pig Farm Campsite.*

*On the way up, we met two couples. One of the gentlemen had on a T-shirt that said "Undignified," with the Bible reference from where the phrase came from. We stopped to talk to him and asked what church he was with because of his shirt. Seems that we were two of the few people who had ever understood what the saying on his shirt referred to—it was the title of a David Crowder Band song. We chatted about the youth ministry at his church in Roanoke, Virginia and I told him that I had done sound with the David Crowder band and that we still kept in touch. The other couple was from Liberty University in Lynchburg, Virginia, near where my parents live. As we stood as close to the edge of McAfee Knob as the stiff winds would safely allow, we had to agree that the claims of this stately overlook having the best views in Virginia was by no means understated. We could see all the way to Roanoke and everywhere you looked, the views took your breath away."* - Windtalker & Mom

As unbelievable as McAfee Knob and its views were, our chance encounter with these folks from Roanoke and Liberty really enriched our day. Meeting them reinforced our desire to take every opportunity to share life and our faith with people we met, with our families, and with the other people we loved back home.

*August 18th:*

*"Almost five full months into our adventure and each day*

*still brings with it moments of unexpected and unbelievable occurrences. We were clawing our way up the twin peaks of "The Kinsmans" and discovered that, not only were these mountains just a glimpse of the romantically-agonizing hike that was to come, but that strangers on the trail could so dramatically impact our lives. Although today's trek was only 8.8-mile long, it was physically arduous and took a full eight hours to complete. First, we climbed Mt. Kinsman's south slope to 4,358 feet—two hours of technical climbing up boulder faces. We had to clutch onto roots and trees lining the trail in order to make any amount of vertical headway and to keep from sliding back down the slope. Near the summit, we took a welcomed snack break on a rock ledge overlooking the indescribably expansive valley below.... As emotionally overwhelming as the views around us were, the most emotional moment of the day came as we scaled a very long, narrow, steep, and difficult section.*

*Halfway up we encountered a large group of day-hikers on their way down. They inquired as to whether or not we were thru-hikers and when we confirmed we were, they stepped aside to let us pass—and applauded us until we were out of sight. It was at that moment that we became fully aware of what we were in the midst of accomplishing and how inspirational our adventure was for other people. More importantly, little did these day-hikers know how much their appreciation of what we were doing bolstered our spirits and positively affected the level of dedication Mom and I felt for each other. At that moment, we also sensed that doing this odyssey together was as important as whether or not we succeeded in completing it. The individual sense of joy we felt was superseded by our shared joy in living that defining moment."* - Windtalker & Mom

Even to this day, as we hike other trails, our trail family continues to grow. In 2009, as we hiked from Smugglers Notch to Jeffersonville on Vermont's Long Trail, we spent several wonderful days traveling with two brothers, "Ho" and "Hum." Thrown into each other's company by time, the weather, and a mutual passion to conquer the ruggedness of this oldest of long-distance trails, we shared each others lives, assisted each other up steep and dangerously slippery precipices, and grew to become friends.

*People are the Trail.* There is an unmistakable duality to that statement. Be it the Appalachian Trail or the trail of life, the love and compassion we show to our fellow *travelers* should be the same. The selflessness and uncompromising humanity we all became part of on the A.T. is what real life should also be about. Our incredible journey was bereft of judgment, confrontation, criticism or disdain for our fellow hiker. Overshadowing any differences between us was the all-encompassing desire to make it successfully to the end of our journey and to assure that everyone else made it as well. Such must be a life of faith—to not only reach the mountaintop of the eternal life set forth for us by God but to also see that everyone else makes it there as well. We are all the *Family of God.*

> *"But you are the ones chosen by God, chosen for the high calling of priestly work, chosen to be a holy people, God's instruments to do his work and speak out for him, to tell others of the night-and-day difference he made for you—from nothing to something, from rejected to accepted." -* 1 Peter 2:9-10 (The Message)

---

## Devotional: *"Family & Community"*

*"Let us not give up meeting together as some are in the habit of doing, but let us encourage one another..." -* Hebrews 10:25

When you *do life* with people, it changes you. When you interact with others on a day-to-day basis, such as in the work place or in your community, you may not know what someone else is going through. Someone may snap at you for no apparent reason and you may react in kind. There is a story I have heard about a person who was riding a train and was getting impatient with a man who was letting his kids loudly run around and act crazy. When he confronted the man, the man shared how his wife had just died and he did not have the strength to confront the kids. As I said, you just never know what people are going through.

On the trail, we all had a good idea of the trials and tribulations we were each facing. Of course, unless someone opened up and shared, we did not know about the pain, suffering, or emotional trauma he or she brought along to the trail. But, we had a pretty good idea of the physical challenges we were each facing. We all knew what our day was like going up the mountains from Stecoah Gap, up Roan Mountain, up Clingman's Dome, down Jug End and down Mt. Greylock. We knew what it was like on the long down from Mt. Madison and both up and down Mt. Katahdin. We knew what it was like to hike in rain, heat, and with hordes of mosquitoes and gnats buzzing about. We also knew about the glorious days above the clouds and the beautiful flowers or animals that caught our eyes. I cannot think of another time in my life where I was sharing the same experience with so many people—where we all knew what it was like—almost without explanation. Plus, we were there to encourage each other! I can say *"Remember coming over Grayson Highlands?"* and Windtalker would *know* exactly want I was referring to. So, it's no surprise that Windtalker and I long to be back out on the trail, sharing the experience together! Why do you think so many previous thru-hikers are out on the trail as trail angels after their experience? Let's not give up meeting each other and encouraging each other in life! – *Mom*

## Prayer

*"Dear Lord, give me the compassion to love those around me as you would love them. Help me be an encourager to everyone I meet on the path."*

# The Walk

*"Wonder is involuntary praise"* - Edward Young

As we traveled the thousands of miles that embody the backbone of the Appalachian Trail, and daily came face-to-face with natural wonders that defy description, we could not help but feel overwhelmed—overwhelmed with sights, sounds, smells and colors so vivid, so lush, so surreal, and so awe-inspiring that no measure of literary eloquence could adequately describe them. Time after time, we were left utterly speechless and a thesaurus was completely inadequate for the task of aptly describing what we experienced.

When we reached the Tennessee and North Carolina border, we had already run out of adjectives to convey the magnitude of what we were seeing, hearing, smelling and feeling. Possibly, only the strains of a powerful symphony could even come close to adequately expressing the totally overwhelming pleasures that stirred within us. Ultimately, we relinquished control of even trying to find the appropriate descriptive words and attributed the joy of each new sensation to it being *A God Thing*. We gave praise and thanks for every day we were out there embracing them. Our sense of wonder was *involuntary praise*.

> Native American Wisdom
>
> *"There are no temples or shrines among us save those of nature. Being children of nature, we are intensely poetical. We would deem it sacrilege to build a house for the One who may be met face to face in the mysterious, shadowy aisles of the primeval forest, or on the sunlit bosom of virgin prairies, upon dizzying spires and pinnacles of naked rock and in the vast jeweled vault of the night sky! A God who is enrobed in filmy veils of cloud, there on the rim of the visible world where our Great-Grandfather Sun kindles his evening campfire; who rides upon the rigorous wind of the north, or breathes forth spirit upon fragrant southern airs, whose war canoe is launched upon majestic rivers and island seas—such a God needs no lesser cathedral."* [15] - Charles Alexander, Ohiyesa, (Dakota Sioux)

Even for those on the trail who claim to have no religious leanings, there is no escaping from the spiritual essence of what envelopes everyone on the trail. Perhaps it is the sight of a peregrine falcon taking flight from its cliff-side perch and then majestically gliding on the breeze into the valley beneath you. Or maybe you find yourself standing on a mountaintop amidst a shroud of fog and then it miraculously blows away to expose miles of meandering trail on the ridgeline ahead of you—a vista, bathed in rays of sunlight cast through a natural prism of the clouds. Sitting on an overlook, sculpted by years of wind and rain, peering at passing clouds as they create an ever-changing palette of greenish hues on the sun-drenched mountains across a valley, every imaginable emotion simultaneously rushes to the surface—each one attempting to take prominence over the others. This confluence of feelings overtakes you, your heart begins to race, your mind and soul go limp, and you feel like a blob of emotional Silly Putty®.

In a story from, *Glimpses of an Invisible God - Experiencing God in the Everyday Moments of Life,* two novice hikers reflect on how experiencing the wilderness provided new meaning to the terms, *praise and worship.*

*"The last hundred yards made up for the previous half-mile of shifting rocks and shirt-snagging underbrush. It was almost as if the mountain had admitted defeat and offered up an easy path to Cindy and Brian. They wove their way to a large flat boulder and climbed onto it.*

*'Wow! Look at that!' Brian exclaimed.*

*The treetops below swayed gently in the breeze. A hawk soared gracefully overhead. Tiny mountain flowers smiled in the sunshine. The rhythm of this natural world was unfamiliar to two college kids weaned on computers and television. Cindy spun slowly to soak up as much as possible.*

*'It's as if all of nature is singing out to the Creator,' she said in awe.*

*Time passed much too quickly, and as they climbed down the rocky path, they were silent. They didn't want to interrupt the most excellent praise and worship service they'd ever experienced."* [16]

The overpowering sense of beauty and awe of these and other spectacles along the A.T. stagger the imagination. What we encountered simply cannot be conveyed using our limited human understanding and vocabulary. The sensory impact of beholding these sights firsthand embeds itself in one's soul, transcending every feeble attempt by photographers, writers and artists to re-create them. More than once we heard hikers cry out, as they crested the last rocky hurdle on a mountain top to stand on the summit and gaze at the views below, *"My God, this is amazing"* or *"Oh my God,*

> ### Native American Wisdom
> *"Whenever, in the course of a day, we might come upon a scene that is strikingly beautiful or sublime—the black thundercloud with the rainbow's glowing arch above the mountain; a white waterfall in the heart of a green gorge; a vast prairie tinged with the blood red of a sunset—we pause for an instant in an attitude of worship."* [17] - Charles Alexander Eastman, Ohiyesa (Dakota Sioux)

*I can not believe how beautiful this is!"* To the non-Christians, such statements were probably pronounced as nothing more than off-handed, idiomatic responses to what they were experiencing. Yet unbeknownst to them, the sense of wonder that predicated them making such heart-felt statements was in itself praise.

With each passing day and mile on the trail, all the age-old scientific hypotheses on the origin of the universe seemed to matter less and less. This creation we were all standing in, on, and sometimes under, was much too complex and astoundingly wondrous to be the result of chance, evolutionary formula or genetic transformation. In all of humankind's attempts to logically or scientifically explain how the universe came to be, we attempt to make sure that the creation equation is under our control. We need the explanation of the universe's genesis and maturation to be logical—capable of being grasped by our finite knowledge of time and space, and the limits of our rational minds. We simply cannot believe that the explanation of creation could be enigmatic and simply beyond our comprehension. The answer must be within the realm of our comprehension, so we tailor the evolution equation so the answer comes out accordingly. And yet, to believe that creation was the result of a single momentous scientific event in time, as Sir Fred Hoyle, one of the most famous creationists of this century noted, *".....is comparable with the chance that a tornado sweeping through a junkyard might assemble a Boeing 747."* He goes on to say that creation itself, like the 747, requires an "Intelligent Designer."

On our hike, Mom and I witnessed first hand a unique form of "intelligent design" that drives home this point in a fathomable way.

*"One morning in Vermont, we started with a leisurely walk around Little Rock Pond. We loved how they called lakes "ponds" in Vermont, but in relation to the enormity of the mountain landscapes, I suppose they were just ponds. We stopped and chatted with the campsite caretaker and remarked about the pristine location she had at which to spend the summer—a gorgeous pond, a musical stream nearby, cool breezes, and abundant wildlife visible at every turn. Abruptly, we came to the edge of that pond and found ourselves strolling through a beautiful and stately pine forest. The intense aroma in the air, that made it smell like Christmas, overwhelme, us. Purely by accident, I took my eyes off my feet long enough to peer off to the right of the trail where I spotted several large rocks with smaller rocks piled on top of them. Strange, I thought! Just as I noticed these peculiar cairns, I heard Mom exclaim,*

*'Oh wow, you have to see this!'*

*I came around a large rock pile to where she was standing, and there on the ground, were dozens of various-sized piles of rocks, sculpted by hikers who previously passed through that spot. It was a remarkably whimsical sight. Each pile looked like a small gnome and it was as if we had stumbled into some mythical fairy tale land. We walked another quarter mile and there the trail went through another area about thirty square yards covered with more of these stone creations. They were all different sizes and configurations and there were even rocks up in the branches of the trees. Over in one corner, a "peace sign" had been formed on the ground, perhaps made by some "child of the sixties" hiker who had passed this way. The massiveness of the surrounding forest became insignificant as our eyes and piquing imaginations became fixed on the community of small stone statuettes scattered as far as the eye could see. We sensed the trees and boulders surrounding this rock garden were there solely to keep watch over and protect their diminutive stone companions."* - Windtalker & Mom

We regularly joke about seeing things like this rock garden in the woods by saying *intelligent designer*. One need only experience the world of the wilderness, the profoundly intricate and overpowering mystery of the planet on which we live, to realize that it is all more than could be created by accident or by anything we could either comprehend or create. The more knowledge we gain about the complexities of the universe, the more obvious it becomes that our long-held beliefs and hypotheses do nothing more than support the notion of a power larger and more incomprehensible than ourselves. Believing in an *intelligent designer* becomes a more feasible explanation. Those, whose lives were lived decades before the advent of scientific theory and anthropological analysis, understood and appreciated this fact. Their spiritual beliefs were the foundation for decisions critical to the continuance of a prosperous and vibrant society.

In an interview with Backpacker Magazine about the making of his PBS series, "The National Parks: America's Best Idea" filmmaker Ken Burns talks about the spiritual aspects of the series' first episode, "The Scripture of Nature."

*"The language that everyone used, including Abraham Lincoln, who first authorized Yosemite, was the rhetoric of the Bible. That's why we named the first episode, "The Scripture of Nature"—because the national park idea was born from people who were talking about finding God in nature. I don't know whether I would call it God. But I know there's a moment when you feel like you are seeing everything new. There is a vivifyingness to everything, a luminosity to the light. Suddenly, things take on a different relationship. You feel a kinship with all things. Those moments are fragmentary at best for most of us, but I have experienced them deeply in Yosemite and Yellowstone, the Grand Canyon, Denali, Glacier and the Everglades."* [18] - Ken Burns

Could it be that this condition we suffer from, this belief that it is "all about us," is what interferes with our understanding of praise and

71

worship? Perhaps it is that many people view "praise and worship" as terms strictly relegated to a religious context. Is it that we do not actively praise and worship at all or is it that we simply do not recognize it when we see it? The bottom line is that praise and worship are integral elements of our society, as Lou Giglio candidly points out in his book, *The Air I Breathe.*

> *"In fact, some of the purest forms of worship are found outside the walls of the church and have no reference to the God of all creation. All you have to do is drop in on a concert at the local arena or take in a sporting event at a nearby stadium to see amazing worship. People are going for it: lifting their hands, shouting with joy, staking their claim, standing in awe and declaring their allegiance."* [19]

People, who stand at the summit of Mt. Katahdin, Mt. Washington or Clingman's Dome and gaze at the natural world at their feet, recognize the eternal vastness of the universe. At that moment, I suspect they suddenly feel very *insignificant.* Or, when the trail leaves the sanctuary of the forest on Roan Mountain, in Tennessee, and catapults hikers onto the lush, grassy balds of the Roan Highlands, at over 5,000 feet, where they can relish the 360 degree views of the valleys and tip-toe through a herd of huge, free-roaming steers, chances are they develop a propensity for, and appreciation of, the spiritual. It is difficult, if not futile, when surrounded by such natural beauty, to deny the existence of a higher power or as the Native Americans call it, *The Great Spirit.* It is not only the spiritual connection between our natural surroundings and a higher power that is sometimes difficult to make, it can also be those moments of human interaction that, upon reflection, prompt us to offer up praise for the *unexplainably remarkable.* For us, one such interaction took place as we neared the end of our journey.

> *It was only weeks before the end of our thru-hike. On this day, two lives would intersect in an emotional and memorable way. We finished our mountain of pancakes at Harrison's Pierce Pond Cabins and bid our host, Tim Harrison, a fond farewell. It was only three miles to one of the unique "milestones" of the trail—the Kennebec River. Here we made a river crossing in a canoe piloted by Steve Longley, who has ferried hikers from one side of the river to the other for many*

*years....Before piling into the canoe with our gear, we filled out and signed a liability waiver, holding Steve harmless should something unexpected happen on the trip across. After looking at Mom's trail name on her release, Steve emotionally commented on how ironic it was that he was ferrying Mom across the Kennebec River on this particular day. You see, on this very day, just one year before, Steve's own mom had passed away. Seeing Mom's trail name brought thoughts of his mother rushing back. What were the chances we would be at this place, on this day, and be able to share such an emotional and memorable moment with someone we had just met? It was "unexplainably remarkable."* – Windtalker & Mom

J.R. "Model T" Tate, who we had the sincere pleasure of thru-hiking with and who has remained a good friend, told of his perspective on the spiritual nature of the trail and his inability to adequately describe the magnitude of the wonder around him. In his book, *Walking on the Happy Side of Misery,* he describes a time when he stood on a mountaintop, unable to verbalize what he was seeing and feeling, so he lifted his hands to the skies and simply shouted,

*"The heavens declare the glory of God; the skies proclaim the work of his hands."* - Psalm 19:1 (NIV)

*"If someone doesn't believe in God, just have them stand on top of a mountain and look out at all of creation in wonder."* – Model T

In life, there are many times when no matter how hard you try, what you plan and what you envision as the outcome of that plan, just never materializes. This was a reality of the trail that we reluctantly learned very early on in our thru-hike. All the detailed plans, lists and itineraries we spent months creating, and deemed essential to us succeeding, lasted about four days before being cast aside to be forever stored in the archives of our trip. We resolved ourselves to becoming flexible, letting the weather, terrain, and how we were physically and emotionally feeling, dictate our plans for each day. The only factor that could not be altered was that we had to be at Baxter State Park, in Maine, before it closed in October. As it turned out, all of those things now determining our plans, things over which we had no control, made for more rewarding experiences than we could have ever imagined. Could it be that there was a higher power with other plans for us?

*April 30th:*

*"What a day! 400 miles down and counting! We woke up to windy, overcast skies and intermittent showers, said our goodbyes to Norman the cow, our constant campsite companion last night, and continued our trek north. Our goal was now to start limiting ourselves to twelve-mile days in order to save our feet for the grueling hike into Damascus, Virginia. What we soon found was that today's section of trail was "relatively" flat. Our plan to slow down immediately took a back seat to getting to Damascus as soon as possible.*

*We arrived at Moreland Gap way ahead of schedule, so we decided to have our dinner for lunch and then make the march to Kincora Hostel, where we knew everyone else was headed for the night. We had read such wonderful things about Kincora and its hosts, Bob and Pat Peoples, (sadly, Pat passed away in 2008) that we simply had to stay there and experience it for ourselves...Kincora Hostel was still a good distance away, so to conserve our energy for the final leg of our journey there, we stopped every fifty-five minutes for a five-minute break. We agreed that at 6:30 pm we would see how much further we still had to go and then make our decision as to where to spend the night. At 6:30 pm, we were only a 0.2-mile road walk from Kincora so we made our way up the road only to discover that the hostel was already full to overflowing. Our plans had been dashed and to say we were disappointed was an understatement! Those feelings of disappointment exposed just how tired and hungry we were. Our feet also ached after doing almost eighteen miles. Experiencing first-hand one of the landmarks of the trail would simply have to wait for another day. Thoroughly dejected, we headed back to where the trail crossed the road and then begrudgingly dragged ourselves another 0.3 mile to the Laurel Forks Hostel and Conference Center. What a glorious surprise! The place was wonderful. We had the entire bunkhouse to ourselves, in addition to the showers and washer/dryer. The proprietors opened the store so we could* *buy some snacks and we even had a hiker kitchen to use in the morning to make breakfast—all this for $6.00/person and $2.50 to do laundry. Our spirits were lifted! Located right along the Laurel Forks River, with its rumbling waters harmoniously cascading over and around an endless collection of formidable boulders, it was like heaven on earth. Any animosity we felt about not being able to stay at Kincora was remarkably washed away by the lodge's picturesque location and its hospitable staff."* – Windtalker & Mom

Our plan had been superseded by God's plan, giving us more than our share of reasons for praise and worship.

Though we knew it before we ever stepped foot on the Appalachian Trail, when we reached the final summit on Mt. Katahdin, we were even more convinced of the presence of a higher power—God. For six months our prayers had been answered (except for maybe the ones asking that the mosquitoes in New Jersey disappear or that we would see a moose) so there were ample reasons for praise. Even our non-believing friends would occasionally offer up their own off-handed praise as they wearily hobbled into camp just before sunset and exclaimed, *"Thank God, we made it!"*

> *"So you'll go out in joy,*
> *you'll be led into a whole and complete life.*
> *The mountains and hills will lead the parade,*
> *bursting with song.*
> *All the trees of the forest will join the procession,*
> *exuberant with applause.*
> *No more thistles, but giant sequoias,*
> *no more thorn bushes, but stately pines—*
> *Monuments to me, to God,*
> *living and lasting evidence of God."* - Isaiah 55:12 (The Message)

We could certainly say it was easy to be praiseful when everything around us was beautiful, when we had shed all of our worldly responsibilities, when the stress of day-to-day living in the real world became non-existent, and when we were cut off from the disastrous and discouraging news that filled the airwaves and newspapers. But, what about when our hike was completed and we were forced back into our workaday lives? Would we be able to continue to feel God's presence at every turn and be able to still praise and worship him as unabashedly as we had on the trail?

Where we were, what we were doing and seeing, and simply being blessed with the opportunity, finances and health to thru-hike the A.T., were reasons enough for us to praise God. However, when our journey was over, would we be able to draw the necessary spiritual parallels between our adventure and our real lives—parallels that would keep us focused on God and increasingly faithful to His influence in our lives? Would we now look at the world through the kaleidoscope of our spiritual revelations from the trail? How would we apply what we learned and experienced there to the realities that would assail us at home—the very same realities we left behind six months earlier. Realities that challenged our faith then and would, no doubt, challenge us in the future.

Now we are back home—no more glorious windswept vistas, no more clear, cool and serene mountaintop lakes, and no more sitting around a campfire at dusk, with friends and family, recounting our individual exploits of the day. No more being enfolded in the majestic security of God's own wilderness design. Apprehension, not necessarily about God's existence per se, but more so about his level of involvement and control over situations, begin to re-surface as we are confronted with the unexplainable and seemingly random pain and suffering of people all over the world. How can we see God's hand in the beauty all around us when that beauty is shrouded in fear, poverty, hate and carbon monoxide? With so many heart-wrenching scenarios playing out around us, how can we offer up the same level of praise and worship as we did when we were engulfed in the indescribable beauty of the trail and repeatedly witnessed God's unmistakable hand in it? It is a dilemma of faith that has plagued humankind for thousands of years, and many a theologian has attempted to make sense of it. Will we, like Job, be able to?

Job was a man who lived in Uz. He lived righteously, was a man of his word, was devoted to God and hated evil. Job believed so strongly in the protective power of God that God allowed Satan to challenge Job's faith.

*"God said to Satan, 'Have you noticed my friend Job? There's no one quite like him—honest and true to his word, totally devoted to God and hating evil.'*

*Satan retorted, 'So do you think Job does all that out of the sheer goodness of his heart? Why, no one ever had it so good! You pamper him like a pet, make sure nothing bad ever happens to him or his family or his possessions, bless everything he does—he can't lose! But what do you think would happen if you reached down and took away everything that is his? He'd curse you right to your face, that's what.'*

*God replied, 'We'll see. Go ahead—do what you want with all that is his. Just don't hurt him.'"* - Job 1: 8-12 (The Message)

God progressively removed His protection, allowing Satan to take Job's wealth, his children and his physical health and, in so doing, tempt Job to curse God. Yet even through all of this destruction of Job's life, never once did he blame God for his circumstances—in fact, just the opposite was true.

*"Job got to his feet, ripped his robe, shaved his head, then fell to the ground and worshiped: 'Naked I came from my mother's womb, naked I'll return to the womb of the earth. GOD gives, GOD takes. God's name be ever praised.'*

*Not once through all this did Job sin; not once did he blame God."* - Job 1:20-22 (The Message)

David Crowder, leader of the hugely successful Christian band, "The David Crowder Band," suggests in his book, *Praise Habit – Finding God in Sunsets and Sushi,* that there may be more to our reluctance to praise than simply the crush of life that oftentimes casts a heavy shadow over our ability to finding God in the obvious.

*"We naturally understand praise. As kids, we talk about our favorite toys; later we praise pizza and football players. Kids just know how to enjoy things. They give themselves fully to whatever has a hold on them. Remember as a child how we could fearlessly hold up our favorite toy and petition anyone who was in close proximity to behold it?*

*'Look, Mom, look!'*

*We instinctively knew what it was to praise something. It's always been with us. We were created for it. It's a part of who we are. Kids are fabulous at it. But as adults we become self-conscious and awkward. Something gets lost. I think we do it to each other. At some point, I hold the toy up exultantly and you comment that it looks ridiculous to hold up a toy in such a way. It's not a cool toy like I believed it to be. It's worn and tired, you point out. And we slowly chip away at each other's protective coatings of innocence until one day we wake up and notice we are naked and people are pointing...The moment I see a hill painted in greenest of grass, with long infinite blades waltzing in the wind, and make up my mind to sprint to the top, to give myself to gravity and let it roll me down, I hear, 'Dork!' shouted from behind me somewhere and I stop.*

*'What would they think? This is the thing of children. This is not civilized. Act your age.'*

*This is what we have done to one another. When was the last time you played with your food? I used to blow bubbles in my chocolate milk and nibble my Kraft American cheese singles into the shape of Texas. I don't anymore."* [20]

God was in the peace and beauty of the wilderness. We saw and felt it everywhere and every day there were many obvious reasons to offer praise and thanksgiving. At home, His presence often is not as obvious when we search for Him and try to compare our relationship with Him during our wilderness experience—but many similarities do exist. The context in which these similarities exist requires a more profound test of faith and a more open and reflective heart. Because we saw the evidence of God each day during our hike, did not mean that when we returned home He remained in the sovereign refuge of the wilderness he created, leaving the rest of the world to fend for itself. God is, was, and will always be everywhere. It is merely the limit of our understanding and our human perspective that clouds our spiritual vision making seeing and praising Him difficult, if not sometimes, seemingly impossible.

*"Praise is response. Praise happens when there is revelation, and there is revelation waiting around every bend, in places we would not suspect. Our task is to live with our eyes wide*

*open to God's greatness because when we see the imprint of the Creator, our insides will swell with devotion, our hearts will erupt with thankfulness. You will live, breathe and radiate praise. The habit isn't in learning how to praise; it is in reminding yourself who to praise."* [21] - David Crowder

So, how does one transfer the daily praise response learned on the A.T., where one spends six months in a literal social/economic vacuum, free from the cultural influences that get in the way of spiritual growth and having the freedom to openly praise and worship, to life in the real world? Here are some of the things we learned from our time on the trail that now serve us well and help us keep things in a Christian perspective.

- There is much to be thankful for in the small things; sunrises, sunsets, the songs of birds, the smell of wet dirt after a spring shower, etc. The big things always seem to fade away but the small, most important things, remain in your soul forever.
- Do not get angry at God because you do not understand what He is doing. You probably do not understand what a mechanic is doing when he is tuning up your car but you don't get angry at him, do you?
- Never ask, *"God, where are you?"* Just look around and you will see his presence everywhere. Remember to stop talking long enough to hear His voice saying, *"I am here, where are you?"*
- Give praise for the opportunity to meet God face-to-face in every situation, be it good or bad.
- Learn to discern between "needs" and "wants" and believe that God will fulfill the "needs." The "wants" are generally not necessary for survival or happiness. *"Just what I need"* is always enough—*"Just what I want"* is never enough.
- Life is a journey. Keep your eyes always scanning the horizon, your ears always turned to the heavens, your feet always moving, your heart always open and your soul always longing to be filled with new experiences, wonders and memories. This is God's gift to you.

In her book, *When Prayers Are Not Answered,* Elizabeth Rockwood tells of reading a book by Charles Whiston, professor emeritus at The

Church Divinity School of the Pacific in Berkeley, California. In his book, Whiston tells of a life-changing encounter with the Creator.

*"Can we remember times in our own past when we knew beyond all doubting that we were in the presence of the invisible God? I would share...one such time in my life...I had spent two weeks camping in the Adirondack mountains of northern New York...[One night] about two o'clock, I found myself suddenly fully awake...For some hours I walked or sat by the lake, the full moon lighting everything softly. I saw no vision, I heard no voice, but I knew beyond all doubt that an invisible presence which I knew to be God was confronting me. Without words I received the message from God: I was to resign my work with the cotton mills in Boston and...become a minister of Jesus Christ. There was no emotional excitement. I was as still within as nature was without."* [22]

This does not mean that everyone who hears the whisper of God in the wilderness will necessarily be called to ministry. However, it does drive home the point that there is a plan for each of our lives if we only pray for the understanding to recognize it and offer praise when we accept and pursue it.

To hike the Appalachian Trail and live life in a new, uncluttered, and spiritual way allowed us to pursue life with an entirely new perspective and set of tools. The lessons learned, the relationships developed, and the opportunities to experience God's presence in a completely new way, can be carried over into the life that God set out for us. Each real-life event can now be viewed through the memories of time on the trail and what was learned there. Those profound memories and enlightening experiences can be translated into how we react to everyday events, providing reasons for praise. Moreover, when we find those memories and times of enlightenment fading and our spiritual compasses beginning to falter, we take a moment to return to the roots of our spiritual awakening—the natural wonders all around us. Seek out the visible and familiar signs of God's presence—the signs that are all around us if we simply open our eyes and hearts and look.

*"When Robert looked back on his childhood, one of his favorite memories was of his dad's impromptu celebrations.*

*He'd wake the kids in the middle of the night, bundle them up in old sleeping bags and then take everyone out to the backyard to watch a meteor shower. He'd interrupt dinner for a sunset or turn off the TV mid-program to redirect everyone's attention to the lightning flashing over the mountains. He'd halt a family hike to watch a line of ants carry leaves three times their size across the path. But, no matter what natural wonder happened to be taking place, his dad always said the same thing—'Thank you, God!'*

*Pausing to appreciate a work of art in a museum is a natural response to creativity and beauty. So is taking time to appreciate the incredible world God has made. His handiwork is everywhere. Today, why not take a walk or a drive in search of often-overlooked miracles?"* [23]

---

## Devotional: *"Praise"*

*"The heavens declare the glory of God; the skies proclaim the work of his hands."* - Psalm 19:1

I'm sure I am not alone in experiencing moments on the trail such as these:

- Stopping in quiet amazement to watch a bear or rattler (or maybe you saw a moose, we didn't).
- Standing speechless above the clouds on a mountaintop!
- Writing in your journal and running out of adjectives to describe the wonders of the day.
- Stopping to take a photo to record the moment digitally because you never want to forget it (though you still have to remember the wind, breeze, rain, heat, emotion of the moment).
- Standing on top of a high point, and being able to look back at the mountaintops you hiked for the past week.
- Falling. Getting up again, and again, to continue on.

I found myself, more times than not, when experiencing one of these moments, thinking of how amazing God is! How many times, when words failed, did I just think to myself about the fact that here was one more "God thing" to note? I couldn't keep track of how many times that happened. I treasure the opportunities I had every day for six months to see and revel in the glories of God. How could I not? – *Mom*

## Prayer

*"I have seen you Lord – in the beauty and wonder of your creation! I have been blessed by your guidance and protection in times of trouble. I look to you when I am on the mountaintop and when I am in need and you are there! You are an awesome God."*

# Chapter Six

# Materialism versus Simplicity

*"There must be more to life than having everything."* -
Maurice Sendak

If we were all to be excruciatingly honest, many one of us would say that our goals in life revolve around a single driving force—the acquisition of possessions and status. It is a human condition that permeates virtually every decision we make, and every social and moral position we take. It is taught to us from the time we are able to first grasp the concept of "keeping up with the Joneses." The media relentlessly inundates us with advertisements that reinforce the idea that we *need* to have an item in order to be happier, healthier and successful, or even to get that pretty brunette sitting at the local bar we frequent after work. Some would argue that a nice home and a new car are not really possessions but <u>necessities</u>— things that are required in order to live a happy, safe, and productive life. And obviously, having a status-imbued and high-paying job becomes a requirement in order to obtain and maintain

> ### Native American Wisdom
>
> *"To us, as to other spiritually-minded people in every age and race, the love of possessions is a snare and the burdens of a complex society a source of needless peril and temptation. It is a simple truth that we Indians did not, so long as our native philosophy held sway over our minds, either envy or desire to imitate the splendid achievements of the white race. In our own thought we rose superior to them! We scorned them, even as a lofty spirit absorbed in its own task rejects the soft beds, the luxurious food, the pleasure-worshipping dalliance of a rich neighbor. It was clear to us that virtue and happiness are independent of these things, if not incompatible with them."* [24] - Charles Alexander Eastman, Ohiyesa (Dakota Sioux)

these *necessities*. We have bought into these rationalizations hook-line-and-sinker—despite their toll on our psychological, emotional, spiritual and physical well-being. These rationalizations affect the stability of our relationships, often leading to their disintegration. Through our reputation and our possessions, we fall victim to a false sense of security.

The technological advances and never-ending mélange of products touted as the panacea to making our modern lives simpler and us happier, appear to do just the opposite. Yes, we have access to an infinite amount of valuable information via our computers. Yet, the deluge of information we receive forces us to spend inordinate amounts of time sifting through it all—time we could be spending enjoying the simpler things in life. As Ken Jackson, Pastor of Spiritual Formation at Cedarbrook Community Church in Clarksburg, Maryland so aptly points out in his course, *Simplicity - Making Space for God,*

> *"Email, cell phones, the internet and TV allow too many voices to call for our attention and the complexity of modern life forces us to make too many choices each day—demanding that we decide which are important and which are not. Oftentimes, we find this process impossible so everything becomes important. Modern life, technologically-speaking, is anything but simple."* [25]

Vernon Cooper, an elder of the Lumbee tribe of North Carolina, succinctly describes the folly of our technological age in a way that only the wisdom of a Native American can communicate.

> *"These days people seek knowledge, not wisdom. Knowledge is of the past; wisdom is of the future."* [26]

When we began our six-month sojourn, it took a while for us to get used to not having a computer readily available to check emails and to be able to catch up with the latest news on TV whenever we wanted to. At first, not having these things and the other conveniences of home appeared to be monumental, insurmountable sacrifices. However, as the weeks and months on the trail flew by, the need for them discernibly slipped from our consciousness and eventually we began to wonder why we made such a fuss about having them in the first place. We were gloriously free of all the media debris and technological gadgets and we found that, not only were we relieved of an enormous amount of needless stress, but that we were much happier without all of it. This was only one aspect of our education in the meaning and acceptance of a life of simplicity. Our deliverance from the grasp of materialism was just beginning. In our book, *Solemates – Lessons on Life, Love and Marriage from the Appalachian Trail,* we pointed out the joy of discovering the benefits of this wonderful phenomenon.

*"I am a bit of a news junkie and that may be putting it mildly. My car radio is always tuned to the local 24-hour news station and staying up to watch the 11:00 p.m. news chronically results in a rather lethargic next morning. I can never wait until the local newspaper arrives, though it is usually wet or partly destroyed by the elements by the time I get to it. Mom, on the other hand, could care less about the news and relies on my detailed, blow-by-blow accounts of the ghastly events I hear or read about. However, an interesting phenomenon took place not long after we hit the trail on Springer Mountain and it had both of us rethinking the real need to know what was going on in the world.*

*When we were thru-hiking, we quickly acquired a mindset of single-minded purpose. We got up, ate, walked, stopped to eat again every two hours or so, continued walking, ate dinner, and then went to sleep. It sounds rather mundane when you actually write about it. However, in essence, it was the paradigm shift that everyone on the trail adopted in order to successfully complete their wondrous, and oftentimes, torturous journey. For days at a time, we were completely cut off from civilization with all of its negative cultural, social, and political influences and it was seldom that we ever verbally communicated that we wondered what was going on in the world. It was a wonderfully refreshing and stress-free way to exist. The affects of world commerce in turmoil, wars and rumors of wars, pestilence (other than the mosquito attacks in New Jersey), terror attacks, or the death of a famous person or two, found no interested audience on the A.T. Their influence on our lives was negligible, at best, and the bottom line was that our lives were more carefree and we were all better off for not knowing what was going on. Now granted, not hearing news put a huge crimp in my topics of conversation. But there were so many things to see and experience every day, that not hearing the news of a suicide bombing somewhere in the world allowed us the unimpaired freedom to experience the wonder of our surroundings—free of any dark media cloud interfering with our joy. Short of a nuclear attack on the U.S., what was happening in the world was of little consequence to us and had absolutely no affect on how we spent our days. When our time was filled with the wonders of nature, astounding views, and the sounds of a lone moose hightailing it through a stand of saplings only yards from where we stood, the ills of the world were of little relevance. It was transforming! Even now, as I am writing, the nation is communally grieving the loss of thirty-two college students at the hands of an emotionally tormented gunman and I find myself longing for the solace of the trail once more. Some would call such an approach to life escapism, but for all of us that called the A.T. our sanctuary for so many months, it was a quixotic freedom.*

*Everyone, at least once in their life, should go to a place where they are cut off from all civilized forms of communication—no television, radio and no cell phones— and simply experience the pure joy and relaxation of not knowing, and more importantly, not caring about what is going on in the world. Those endless lists of things that one cannot change and that ultimately have no lasting affect on how one pursues their own life, find no home on the trail."* –
Windtalker & Mom

It is indeed a sad state of affairs that we are seldom satisfied with what we have, no matter how much of it we have. It seems that our inborn sense of happiness has been short-circuited. The influx of technology and media hype has us convinced that in order to be happy and satisfied we first need to acquire *stuff*. Jesus warned us about having such a mind-set.

> *"Then he said to them, "Watch out! Be on your guard against all kinds of greed; a man's life does not consist in the abundance of his possessions."* - Luke 12:14-16 (NIV)

Then, not only do we need *stuff* but we need the latest and greatest *stuff*. A perfectly good standard color television is deemed passé and must be replaced with a 40-inch flat screen and then, as if most people can actually see the difference, one has to upgrade to high definition. Each status upgrade brings with it a higher price tag. With this comes an increase in one's credit card debt, resulting in higher monthly payments and interest charges. To meet these financial demands, we work longer hours or look for a more lucrative form of employment in order to cover the additional debt. It is seldom that anyone in this position can give you a logical justification for doing such a thing— everyone just seems to accept it as the normal progression of one's journey on the road to personal happiness, not to mention the means by which to maintain a socially acceptable position near an ever-heightening bar of status. What's more, we will steadfastly proclaim that, *"I'm not like that"* or *"I've earned it"* while sitting on our new leather sofa surfing 300 channels of HD television

> Native American Wisdom
>
> *"It has always been our belief that the love of possessions is a weakness to be overcome. Its appeal is to the material part, and if allowed its way it will in time disturb the spiritual balance for which we all strive."* [28] - Charles Alexander Eastman, Ohiyesa (Dakota Sioux)

on our 5.1 surround-sound home theater system, possessions that are yet to be fully paid for.

> *"Worship money, become a greedy person. Worship sex, become a lustful person. Worship power, become a corrupt person. Worship Jesus, become a Christlike person. We become what we worship."* [27] – Don Williams

What if we could turn this self-defeating, stress-inducing, consumer mind-set completely around to where those who were the happiest with the least were held in the highest regard and would be awarded the highest social status? Those with the most material possessions would then be relegated to a position of social inferiority and would be considered a blight on civilization. What if the new paradigm of *keeping up with the Joneses* meant that you concentrated all your efforts on trying to be as happy as your neighbors, with what little you possessed, and considered the quest of fame and fortune an obstacle to doing so? This is not to suggest that those pushing shopping carts full of items they collected from dumpsters to their cardboard-box homes in some trash-strewn alley would suddenly be elevated to the status of the socially elite. Their situation is at the complete other end of the spectrum and one would be hard pressed to find a homeless person who is remotely content with their lot in life—nor would anyone who is homeless wish their lifestyle on another. Living a life free from the quest for possessions comes down to choice, and for these poor souls, the choice is not usually theirs to make; it is a life of simplicity born of poverty. But such is not the case with most of us. As pointed out in Carl Honore's bestseller, *In Praise of Slowness – Challenging the Cult of Speed,* we can make a voluntary choice to live slower, simpler lives. For Mom and me, that choice was the result of our life-changing hike on the Appalachian Trail—an event that put everything into the correct perspective.

*"We buy things we don't need, with money we don't have, to impress people we don't like."* – Dave Ramsey

When all of us were growing up, there were numerous times, more times than we can probably count, when we were asked,

*"So what do you want to **BE** when you grow up?"*

Because we are brought up with the mistaken belief that our identity hinges on the premise that *"we are what we do,"* most people answer with a list of "occupations" they intend on pursuing. The question asked really implied,

*"So what do you want to **DO** when you grow up?"*

When one honestly thinks about this, would it not be more interesting, and eternally more fulfilling, if our answer to the question, *"What do you want to **BE** when you grow up?"* was,

*"I want to be happy and bring joy to others,"*

*"I want to be loved and be content with what I have and with who I am,"*

or even something as simple as

*"I want to live a plain and simple life, free from stress and competition with those around me?"*

These would perhaps be healthier and more fulfilling answers to the question, *"What do you want to **BE** when you grow up."* What a wonderful change in personal focus that would be. For thru-hikers, all these *"I want to BE..."* answers underscore their very existence on the trail. Many have carried the joy of living out the answers on life they discovered on the trail in their lives after leaving the trail. In the final analysis, Doing requires little more than education, talent, and skill. Being requires selflessness, compassion, love, caring, wisdom, intuition, understanding, and peace. When comparing doing with being, which is of more intrinsic and lasting value, and which brings greater happiness and personal fulfillment?

> *"Tell those rich in this world's wealth to quit being so full of themselves and so obsessed with money, which is here today and gone tomorrow. Tell them to go after God, who piles on all the riches we could ever manage—to do good, to be rich in helping others, to be extravagantly generous. If they do that, they'll build a treasury that will last, gaining life that is truly life."* – Timothy 6:17-19 (The Message)

The most refreshing and illuminating aspect of our A.T. thru-hike was in surviving with so little—yet still having all we needed. Every necessity for making it through the day we carried on our backs—all 35 lbs of it—and we were completely happy. (As a humorous sidebar, Chuckie "Funnybone" Veylupek, in an article written for the *Pacific Crest Communicator Magazine*, quipped that *"....the only distinguishing difference between a homeless person and a thru-hiker is Gore-Tex."* Should the U.S. economy collapse, throwing us into another era of depression, the homeless and the thru-hikers will be ready—and we will survive.

What was not provided by simply opening our packs and searching inside, was provided by the environment around us—the sunsets, sunrises, gentle showers, the rustle of chipmunks through the leaves, the perfume of damp pines, or the delicate flight of a hawk. In those few instances where we did not have exactly what we needed, we learned to improvise solutions from what we did have or from what we found around us. There came an undeniable sense of satisfaction in solving a problem using our own wits, a sense of accomplishment we could never experience by simply running to the supermarket, Home Depot or the local outfitter to purchase the solution. No one epitomized this spirit of joyful simplicity more than "Kutsa."

We hiked several times with Kutsa, a young Israeli woman who was married to a movie producer in Canada. When we met her, she

> ### Native American Wisdom
>
> *"Look at me—I am poor and naked but I am the chief of the nation. We do not want riches but we want to train our children right. Riches would do us no good. We could not take them with us to the other world. We do not want riches. We want peace and love."* [29] - Red Cloud (Sioux)

was making her fifth attempt at completing a thru-hike. Unlike most of us, who left the majority of our worldly possessions at home and carried only what was required for our journey, everything Kutsa <u>owned</u> was in her backpack. Over the course of her four previous thru-hike attempts, she had come to realize that she did not need much more than what was on her back in order to have all her needs met. In fact, she reduced her necessities still further by eating only cold food, which kept her from having to carry a stove and fuel. Her focus was on the journey and the people she met, not on what she had or did not have. She was completely happy and comfortable with her minimalist lifestyle and her exuberance over her life choice was both contagious and inspiring.

Pre-Appalachian Trail, our lifestyle at home was somewhat simplistic when compared to many of our neighbors. Our major foray into "low maintenance living" was that, once all our kids had moved out of the house to pursue their own lives, we scaled back our living arrangements—from a single-family home to a modest townhouse. Wanting to spend as much time together enjoying things that were put on hold while our kids were growing up, we dug up all the grass around our home and replaced it with terraced flower gardens so we did not have to spend time maintaining a yard. We allowed nature to take its course and adorn our yard with a colorful array of plants.

*"You can worship whatever you want, but there'll always be a last-minute twist to the story. Whatever you worship, you imitate: whatever you imitate, you become....If you worship "stuff," your life will become material, void of eternal significance."* [30] - Lou Giglio

However, our home life was not all simplicity and devoid of a materialistic bent. Mom and I were inexplicably hurtling headlong toward the threshold of our retirement years, so we had already had half a lifetime of collecting *stuff*. We insisted that the majority of our stuff was still taking up space in our home because it held sentimental value, not because we had any real need for any of it. Either way, it took up an incredible amount of space and required constant dusting. On March 25, 2006, when we locked the door to our home and headed to the Appalachian Trail for six months with all we needed on our backs, all that stuff remained on its respective shelves, or in closets, until we would return and begin dusting it once more.

But a funny thing happened when we arrived home for a brief break upon reaching the A.T.'s psychological halfway point, Harpers Ferry.

We opened the front door of our townhome, tentatively walked inside as if we were sneaking into someone else's home unannounced, and immediately the Spartan life-style we had become accustomed to on the trail met head-on with our previous lifestyle. Everywhere we turned there was *stuff*—photos on end tables, books and magazines on the coffee table, walls and walls of bookcases stuffed with books, some dating back to our years in college, and even to high school, and some things we no longer even recognized. The feeling that overtook us was depressing at the least and claustrophobic at the worst. Why did we still have these things? Did we really need them? Did they add any intrinsic value to our lives or the lives of others? Four days later, as we once again locked the front door and headed back to Harpers Ferry to pick up where we left off, we had both entered into a pact to throw away or give away much of that stuff as soon as our hike was over. In a practical sense, there were also other things that we vowed to change upon our return from our adventure, things that the trail taught us we could do without.

We now limit our purchases of bottled water. We reuse the plastic bottles we already have and fill them with filtered water from our tap. We have drastically reduced the amount of new clothing we purchase and gave away much of what we already owned that we seldom wear. On the trail, the size of our packs determined how much *stuff* we could have. Curiously, our house had been determining how much *stuff* we should comfortably hold onto, not how vital a role that stuff played in our existence. A house should be only as big as you need to be comfortable—the number of possessions you acquire is always in direct proportion to how much space you have in which to house them. We may downsize our living space even further and move into a small apartment. This would force us to clean house again and limit future acquisitions. In addition, by renting, we would have still fewer maintenance responsibilities and, therefore, more time to invest in the joys of life.

> *"Do not store up for yourselves treasures on earth, where moth and rust destroy, and where thieves break in and steal. But store up for yourselves treasures in heaven, where moth and rust do not destroy, and where thieves do not break in and steal."* – Mathew 6:19-20 (NIV)

There are many hikers on the A.T. who, either by conscious choice or because of an inability to reintegrate themselves into the *real world* after their thru-hike, have found the lure of simplicity so mesmerizing and freeing that they have chosen to live on the trail indefinitely. We seemed to run into these same hikers no matter where we were on the trail. I suppose some would call them A.T. hobos—harkening back to the days when men chose a different type of trail and left society behind to live on the rails. For these hikers, there are only brief returns to civilization for short stints of employment so they can purchase the necessary supplies to keep them on the trail for as long as possible. This is a small sacrifice to make in order to continue their wanderlust. Are they happy? The ones we met appeared to be exceedingly so. They shunned the materialistic vortex of society, giving them the time and the freedom to concentrate on the eternal joys of life— relationships, service and creation. Whether they realize it or not, theirs is truly a spiritual journey.

Because I am a musician, my days at home are continually filled with music, so I wondered what it would be like to not have music playing whenever I wanted on the trail. To appease this fear, I brought along a Native American flute for entertainment and playing it brought me more satisfaction, and connection with the natural world around me, than any pre-recorded song. I found that I did not need a surround sound system in order to be absorbed in the beauty of music. The wilderness around me provided more inspiration and solitude than any living room or studio ever could. At times, I was even blessed with a natural amphitheatre in which to serenade other hikers. There were those who did bring music with them programmed into their iPods®, but most found the charging of batteries to be more aggravation than the music was worth. They soon discarded them in exchange for the natural, non-compressed sounds of the wilderness—the wind, the birds, and the rustling of their feet through the leaves on the trail.

Life on the trail forced all of us into a more wholly simplistic lifestyle. Oddly enough though, hiking the trail was not a life-style of acute deprivation. Unless we made a miscalculation on how much food and water we would need to carry us to the next shelter or town, we were rarely without what we needed. There were points, especially early on, when we all vocalized our longing for things we *wanted*. A quick analysis, though, of how acquiring such things would impact our budgets, how much weight an item would add to our packs, and what other necessity we would have to jettison from our packs in order to make room for our *wants*, made such longings short-lived. And, what if we did give in to that burning desire for something we wanted—once we had it, how long would it be before the emotional attachment waned and we could no longer justify carrying it?

Though advertising agencies would like us to believe differently, the truth we learned on the trail was that there are only five basic human needs that actually need to be met in order to be happy: water, food, clothing, shelter, and companionship. That's right! One does not really need to color their hair a certain color that lasts through a week's worth of washings or shave with a specific razor that cuts so close the women simply cannot resist you. You do not even have to use a deodorant that keeps you so fresh and dry that you draw the opposite sex to you like moths to a flame. Five to seven days on the trail without a shower or deodorant, and six months without shaving, was absolute proof that neither was a necessity for happiness. As thru-hikers, it was delightful to be free of the influence and social manipulations of the media, to discover the stress-free joy of having all our needs met in the purest sense. Having spent half of a year refreshingly free from the mindless drone of television, catalogue, and computer advertising insisting that we needed to buy something, we learned we could survive just fine and not fall prey to such repugnant advertising pressure. We also knew that upon our return home, we would now limit how much of this drivel we allowed to permeate our lives and be all the better off for making such a choice.

There was also another interesting benefit to our hike—a footnote to our adventure that was a pleasant and reassuring surprise. By purchasing only the items we needed to survive, with the removal of incessant advertising, and with so many of our normal expenditures now non-existent, such as putting gas in our cars and dining out several nights a week, we actually saved money. Being able to accomplish such a feat, even though we were not working, reinforced the notion that simplicity does not mean forgoing financial stability.

Our days were indelibly marked by the enjoyment of our journey and each other. There was no struggling to acquire more prestigious food, more impressive types of beverages, or a larger and more esteemed model of tent. The streams and rains provided our water. Our meals, though not incredibly creative or exotic, were still quite edible and contained the calories, protein, and other nutrients our bodies needed. Clothing was chosen based on its functionality, durability, and light weight—style was a non-issue. More often than not, hikers would comment on someone's clothing based on how well it "wicked" sweat away, how quickly it dried, or how much warmth it provided when compared to its weight. Having a well-known celebrity endorse a piece of clothing carried about as much weight as did the fact that it cost ten times more than what you were wearing. Cost was no indicator of anything's intrinsic value, be it clothing or equipment. Paying a fortune for a piece of gear did not elevate your status in the hiking community. In fact, hikers generally were more impressed by how little a good-performing piece of gear cost—hiking budgets being what they are.

Hikers' choices of shelter were varied, but were never made based on what other hikers would think. Some exclusively used the shelters along the trail so as not to have to carry a tent at all. Though a bit risky, requiring that one leave camp early and walk fast so as to arrive at a shelter before anyone else, no one who chose to carry a tent ever criticized those who chose not to. A tent had to meet only four criteria: it had to set up and take down fast, it had to keep you and your gear dry, had to be as light as possible, and needed to be just large enough to comfortably fit its occupants. Brand name, color or cost did not impress anyone.

As for companionship, there was no hierarchy on the trail and no references, either real or inferred, as to one's particular social status among the other hikers—though there were occasional references to certain hikers smelling worse than others did. The A.T. put us all on the same level playing field and none of us cared what anyone else's status was in the real world. Though each of us was unique, we were all equal, and never was there any attempt at one-upmanship, except for some good-natured competition as to who covered the most miles in a given day. Getting along, helping and encouraging each other, enjoying each other's company, and concentrating on each other's similarities, rather than differences, allowed us to develop relationships in a very short time. Many of these relationships continue to this day.

Other than needing to arrive at the trailhead for the beginning of our adventure on the correct day, and then having a reference calendar to assure that we would arrive at Baxter State Park before it closed in October, there was no real need for a daily calendar or a strict schedule. More than once, we lost track of exactly which day of the week it was. This was such a contrast to our workaday lives where every moment of every waking hour was marked by an alarm, an entry from an electronic, handheld calendar, a pop-up reminder from

Outlook®, a notation on a calendar, or a fluorescent yellow Post-It® note on the kitchen counter. At home, we ate our meals at precise, prescribed intervals—not necessarily when we were hungry. Moreover, our choice of local TV programming dictated what time we went to sleep—not the fact that we were exhausted and could barely keep our eyes open. Timetables on the trail were refreshingly different and lacked the stress built into our regular schedules. The rhythm of every hiker's day was determined by the sunrise, sunset, thirst, hunger, the quality and accessibility of places to sit to eat meals, and the mileage to the next shelter or campsite—nothing more, nothing less. How wonderful it was to know that, at any given time, wherever we were was where we were supposed to be.

How many people, either by genetic predisposition or simply force of habit, live their lives based on a "to do" list? Fortunately or unfortunately, a perspective generally dictated by personality type, such a list is either mandatory or utterly ludicrous. Often the list centers around activities or things to accomplish on a particular day. For the more Type A driven personalities like Mom and myself, a complete "Life List" or "Bucket List" acts as a road map for the rest of our lives, a constant reminder of our mortality and the shortness of life in which we have to check off each item. An item checked off or crossed out represents an activity completed—a goal attained and a measure of the value of our lives. Our thru-hike offered up a unique opportunity to experience the magic and liberating joy of living without a list. We began our journey with a rather extensive spreadsheet showing all the shelters, towns, restaurants, outfitters, and other essentials along the trail—each with its respective mileage marker and our expected date of arrival. By day four, the trail had inflicted its unpredictability and ruthlessness of terrain on us, rendering our spreadsheet useless. It was quickly relegated to a place of honor in one of our supply boxes.

Our ONLY goal, as was everyone else's, was to reach the summit of Mt. Katahdin. Every other action associated with reaching that goal was just part of the journey. Of course, there were plans each day to make it to a certain shelter or to walk a certain number of miles. But, plans ARE NOT goals. Goals are concrete, immutable, and are characterized and measured by success or failure. Plans on the other hand are malleable, free of time constraints, and are rarely associated with a person's character, nor do they influence a person's level of self-esteem. What was so wonderful about living each day without a list was that it gave us time to think about and discuss other things—

things of infinitely more importance than if we were going to reach a certain destination by a certain time.

Our life on the A.T., with all of its formidable and rewarding experiences, also allowed us to refocus on our journey as Christians—a journey not unlike our hike. The comparisons to a walk of faith were incontrovertible. Nestled within the moments on the trail of joy and sorrow, blue skies and thunderstorms, solitude and challenges, was a simple life—free from all the complexities of a material existence. Those months of simplicity gave us a new clarity of thought and purpose, allowing us to discover the intrinsic, freeing and eternal value of simplicity. Living a life where the grip of materialism has no quarter is one of the very foundations of living a life of faith.

> *"We sometimes talk about the "free will" God has given us as if He has completely cut us loose from Himself. We are not so free. We do not have free will when it comes to eating or not eating. Our very hunger demands that we eat. And our God has built into us certain other hungers. It is possible to live away from God and never hunger for material things. But there comes a time when those material things do not satisfy. We have deeper soul hungers and those hungers are cords by which God has bound our soul."* [31] - Charles Allen

Our journey on this earth, comparable to our hike, is short when compared to the eternal scheme of things. Yet, even as relatively short as our hike was, it was awash with importance and meaning. A life of faith is even more so. The very foundation of being a Christian, being in the world but not of the world, is a difficult, yet essential, tenet. In order to succeed at this responsibility, one must be free of the clutter, both materially and internally, that is a barrier to living the life God wants for us.

> *"So here's what I want you to do, God helping you: Take your everyday, ordinary life—your sleeping, eating, going-to-work, and walking-around life—and place it before God as an offering. Embracing what God does for you is the best thing you can do for him. Don't become so well-adjusted to your culture that you fit into it without even thinking. Instead, fix your attention on God. You'll be changed from the inside out. Readily recognize what he wants from you, and quickly*

*respond to it. Unlike the culture around you, always dragging you down to its level of immaturity, God brings the best out of you, develops well-formed maturity in you."* - Romans 12:1-2 (The Message)

By its very nature, a lifestyle of simplicity, free from the quest for self-importance and material gain, is a slower lifestyle—a lifestyle that allows for the moments of solitude necessary to enjoy life to its fullest. In solitude, we are afforded the opportunities to connect with our Creator and travel the path He has laid out for us. Are we even aware of the problems of a cluttered, simplicity-obstructing life? From the *Simplicity - Making Space for God* course, here are three points to ponder.

I. *We have difficulty relaxing or relishing solitude.* [32] (Simplicity in quiet.)

Unfortunately, in the maelstrom of our current culture, moments of relaxation and solitude are difficult to recognize, and even more difficult to take advantage of. However, the option to do so resides within our sincere desire to extract ourselves from all the techno-adrenaline-induced chaos around us and find space to experience the rewards of thinking—for solitude. It is said that our generation is the "connected generation," brought together by the wonder of cyberspace. Look around and everywhere are multitudes of people with cell phones constantly in hand or Bluetooth® devices attached to their ears like some alien, blue, glowing appendage, each person waiting for the next call—the call that will rescue them from the isolation they have experienced since the last call. And there are those with iPods® constantly feeding excessive decibels of sound through their ear buds in an attempt to subvert any chance of interaction with the world around them or any opportunity to sit quietly, to reflect and observe. Technology has made solitude and reflection a scary, dark, and lonesome place to visit.

But are they truly connected? Yes, they are electronically connected to friends, family and colleagues, but is this obsession with cyber-connectivity an obstruction to their being connected to what is eternally important—their own souls and the loud whispers of *The Creator*? Sadly, these electronic advancements, as ingrained in our society as they are, have many caught up in the allure of the virtual. They have become oblivious to the obvious, detached from the memorable, and uninterested in the endearing and the eternal. Technology has stealthily morphed from being a convenience to being an intrusion.

Mom and I had deliberately taken ourselves away from all that superfluous connectivity and celebrated six months of shameless and unencumbered moments of solitude in which to reflect and become one with the world around us. Our return to our regular lives would now include the same types of moments. It would be a conscious choice to do so. As did many others, we carried a cell phone with us on the trail, but it was used only in emergencies or to check on accommodations in towns we were soon to arrive in. In the rare cases when our fellow hikers did need to use their phones, they respected everyone else's privacy and went off, out of earshot, to make their calls.

Even on the A.T., finding moments of solitude were sometimes difficult, especially when staying at a shelter chocked-full of other hikers or when in town for a "zero day," a day to relax, shower and restock our packs. But, most of the time the opportunities for solitude abounded on the trail and if we failed to capitalize on those moments it was our own fault. As often as possible, we made the most of the peace and tranquility offered to us by creation and found those times of relaxation and solitude, to be refreshing and of immense spiritual value.

*March 29th:*

*"Since it was only 3:00 p.m., we decided to hike to the nearby tent site at Poplar Stamp where we planned on having a quiet, and hopefully, romantic evening. Being introverts at heart, or more likely because of genetic disposition, we longed for time alone to recharge our emotional batteries. We did enjoy being around the other hikers but a break from the maddening crowd every so often was a welcome respite. Although we wanted to spend as much time as possible with other hikers and develop the type of trail family bonds that are synonymous with hiking the A.T., we both expressed our desire to be alone—together. Quiet, sunset drenched evenings, sitting under a canopy of tall conifers and discussing not only our journey but blissfully talking about our hopes and dreams for the future, were important ingredients of our grand adventure. It was a time to share our*

*innermost longings and to deepen our relationship. Tonight, we hoped, would be such an occasion.*

*Being less than a week into our journey, our spirits were high and physically we were doing quite well—a few small hot spots had developed on our feet, and we had some cramping, but we were in much better shape than many of our hiking comrades. God was everywhere we looked and the most amazing thing about being out here, besides the number of mountains supporting the trail on their backs, was the quiet. There were no cars, sirens, boom boxes, and only an occasional plane. As we walked, we often would simply stop, breathe as quietly as possible, and listen to just how quiet it was. More than once, the only sound was our heartbeats. It was the type of quiet where even an atheist could not deny the presence of something greater than himself. As dusk began to cast its spell over the surrounding hillsides, it suddenly appeared. There, encircled by a stand of pines whose fallen needles covered the ground in a rich, brown carpet, was the object of our desire—Poplar Stamp Tentsite. It was the romance of the wilderness personified. The air suddenly became still and the sounds of nature cascaded off the trees. This was the type of place that we talked about finding, the type of place that would accentuate our passion for the trail and bolster our passion for each other.*

*Mom unpacked our packs and prepared to make dinner and I was off to get water that was not only quite some distance down the trail, but as I distressingly found out, was less than abundant. I spent an inordinate amount of time digging a pool around the dribbling spring simply to be able to get enough water to fill what containers needed to be replenished. In fact, I was gone so long that "Mom," for the first time, was worried that something had happened to me. However, nothing, not even a struggle to get water, would diminish our longing for this place. It was as if we were preparing for our first date and absolutely nothing was going to stand in the way of it being perfect. As I headed back up the trail to our tent site, I ran into "Cosmic Punchline" and one of the other female hikers on the A.T., his partner "Sherps," who was already nursing such awful blisters on her feet that she had removed her boots and was hiking in her Crocs®.*

*The rest of the evening was a Hallmark® moment, complete with chirping birds, a gentle breeze and romantic conversation. All of this was accentuated by a gorgeous sunset that fluidly resolved itself into a wondrous star-filled sky. We felt closer to each other and to our mutual passion of making our thru-hike a reality than we had ever felt. We were experiencing the complete blessing of being able to chase this dream of ours and anguished over those who do not, or cannot, chase the true desires of their hearts."* – Windtalker & Mom

The good news is that there are other benefits of simplicity that help to overcome the stranglehold that the deluge of societal influences of life have on us.

## II. *Simplicity cultivates the art of letting go.* [33]

Anyone who has done any amount of long-distance backpacking is aware of the benefits of simplicity. They have consciously let go of everything shackling them to an existence defined by material possessions in exchange for one of unbridled, simplistic subsistence—devoid of complexities. They have discovered that freedom is not found in having and doing, but rather in being and experiencing.

For Christians, the opposite of simplicity is not complexity, it is duplicity—a divided heart leads to incompatible priorities.

*"A devout life does bring wealth, but it's the rich simplicity of being yourself before God. Since we entered the world penniless and will leave it penniless, if we have bread on the table and shoes on our feet, that's enough."* – Timothy 6:6-8 (The Message)

*"Don't wear yourself out trying to get rich; restrain yourself! Riches disappear in the blink of an eye; wealth sprouts wings and flies off into the wild blue yonder."* – Proverbs 23: 4-5 (The Message)

By choosing to let go, we become aligned with the values that free us from materialism and all its associated exigency. We are then able to more fully honor God. We found this to be true on the A.T. Every day, without the external and self-induced pressures to excel, we experienced an awakening of our souls. This awakening was brought about, not by what we possessed, but by what we did not possess. This simplicity opened the door for us to focus on the possessions that were truly important—our families, each other, the magnificence of the creation in which we walked, and our relationship with the natural world and its Creator.

> "*Before I go to bed, I like to go by our children's rooms and look at their faces. They are sound asleep, perfectly relaxed, completely at peace. I wonder why the people I've seen today are not like that. Once we did have that peace but as we grow older, our lives become more complicated.*
>
> *We think of the living we have to make, the debts we owe, of what will happen to us in our old age. We worry about the world situation, we get crossed up with other people, we think about the wrongs we have committed, we are afraid for our health. Gradually the peace of our minds is drained away and gone. First, we need to empty our minds. It is impossible to be at peace as long as we hold certain things in our minds.*" [34]
> - Charles Allen

III. *Simplicity is about keeping the main thing the main thing. Doing so brings great freedom.* [35]

Our journey from Georgia to Maine had only one goal, one main thing—reaching Mt. Katahdin before Baxter State Park closed for the season. This goal became an all-encompassing, all-consuming passion made possible by the fact that there were no other outside influences standing in our way. Our lives and our packs were stripped down to the barest of essentials—just what we needed to reach our destiny. There was never a moment when what we possessed in our "real lives" had any bearing on whether we would succeed or not. All that stuff was of no consequence then, and having shunned it, if for only six months, allowed us a freedom to concentrate on our *main thing*. We learned to enjoy the endless array of wondrous things around us without having to own them. In many ways, our ability to keep the summit of Katahdin the *main thing* is analogous to the perspective a Christian must have. It is the very freedom, imparted by simplicity, which helps keep God the "main thing."

*"Yet when I surveyed all that my hands had done and what I had toiled to achieve, everything was meaningless, a chasing after the wind; nothing was gained under the sun."* – Ecclesiastes 2:11 (NIV)

---

## Devotional: *"Simplicity"*

*"Then He said to them, "Watch out! Be on your guard against all kinds of greed; a man's life does not consist in the abundance of his possessions."* - Luke 12:14-16

For the most part, everything I needed was on my back. On the other hand, since we were hiking as a couple and sharing the load, everything that we <u>both</u> needed was in one pack or the other. What a concept!

Now, I find myself regularly asking a number of questions at home. How much stuff do I really need? Do I really need to keep that footlocker of memorabilia from my childhood? Will anyone ever be interested in it but me? Do I need all of those old clothes on the shelf in the basement that do not fit me? Do I really need a new car every 35,000 miles? Do I really need all those shelves of books? Simplicity in my life is not just about the stuff. It is also about my schedule and my thoughts. Does my schedule really need to be filled all the time so that I do not have a moment to breathe? Can I simplify the calendar so that I have more time and room for people? Do I really need to keep so busy? Do I really have to stay so connected with email and have the latest Blackberry® or iPhone® application? Do the questions ever stop?!

So, yes we scaled back on the stuff after the hike. And, in giving some of it away, I'm sure we have blessed others with what we really don't need. But, it is also apparent every day, when we reflect on what simplicity means, that we haven't scaled back enough. Our focus is still too often on our stuff, our shopping list, or our to-do list and our calendar. – *Mom*

## Prayer

*"Lord, help us be mindful that our lives don't revolve around the abundance with which you have blessed us. That possessing things*

*isn't what truly matters. Help us continue to share your gifts with the people whose lives we touch."*

# Chapter Seven  Pride and Humility

*"Humility is the ability to give up your pride and still retain your dignity"* – Vanna Bonta

HUMILITY – noun:   The quality or condition of being humble; modest opinion or estimate of one's own importance, rank, etc.;
HUMBLE – adjective:   Not proud or arrogant;
PRIDE – noun:   Unduly high opinion of oneself.

In this day and age of the relentless pursuit of notoriety and elevated social status, with all its glamorous, garish, and oftentimes extravagant trappings, humility is condemned to the shadows of society as a cultural liability. Humility is recognized as a human quality worthy of envy and appreciation but is also viewed by many as a sign of weakness that cannot readily coexist with the current mores of success. People in the public spotlight, either by design or by fortuitous circumstances, are there because of their burning desire to stand out—to be noticed, adored, envied, and to be modeled after. They long to leave a legacy that will engrain them in the history of politics, sports, the arts, and most importantly, our history as a civilization. Simply to be an honest, moral, caring, humble person is to have a life that is often overlooked, considered by many as having little intrinsic value.

Author Donald Miller, in his book, *Searching for God Knows What,* writes of a television interview he watched in which actor Tom Arnold was promoting his book, *How I Lost Five Pounds in Six Years.*

*"The interviewer asked why he wrote the book and the honesty of his answer was quite amazing. The comedian stated that most entertainers are in show business because they are broken people, looking for affirmation. 'The reason I wrote this book,' Tom Arnold said, 'is because I wanted*

*something out there so people would tell me they liked me.*
*It's the reason behind almost everything I do.'"* [36]

Yet, look at those who did not succumb to the quest for public esteem, but surprisingly found their way there anyway by virtue of the very humility shunned by many of their contemporaries. People like Mother Teresa, Mahatma Gandhi, Abraham Lincoln, and Martin Luther King toiled in humbleness with a clear belief that their humility was of far greater value than their accomplishments. Their desire to preserve their dignity far outweighed any benefits derived from foisting themselves into the limelight, though they often found themselves there. It was the burning desire to preserve their humility at all costs that made them successful and endeared them to their generation and every generation that has come after them. The true litmus test for whether or not a person has truly had an impact on society, living a life of value, is not in what they accomplished but in how well they lived their lives. Neither the ravages of time, nor the politically expedient re-writing of history, will erase the influence that these icons of humility had on other's lives and their reputations will never be called into question because of a pious spirit.

During a conversation with his roommate, Donald Miller also brought up an interesting subject.

*"Let's say I was an alien and I had to go back to my home planet and explain to some head-o-the-aliens guy what people on this planet were like."* [37]

As he worked through how he would describe all the things that make life on this planet unique, and that define the way we live, he filtered his description of humans down to one succinct notion.

*"Humans, as a species, are constantly, and in every way, comparing themselves to one another, which, given the brief nature of their existence, seems an oddity and, for that matter, a waste. Nevertheless, this is the driving influence behind every human's social development, their emotional health and sense of joy, and sadly, their greatest tragedies. It is as though something that helped them function and live well has gone missing, and they are pining for that missing thing in all sorts of odd methods, none of which are working. The greater tragedy is that very few people understand they*

*have the disease. This seems strange as well because it is obvious. To be sure, it is killing them, and yet sustaining their social and economic systems. They are an entirely beautiful people with a terrible problem.*" [38]

It is part of the human condition to aspire to have the best or be the best—to stand out from others so as to make ourselves look and feel special. Children are taught from an early age to be the best, to excel in their studies, in sports and in the arts. The desire to excel is a mandate passed on by parents and by society, be it orally, by example, or sometimes by mere inference. Parents have numerous reasons for pushing. In some instances, it is to prod their children to obtain a better life than they themselves have. Parents who lived through the 1930s, or other historically dark financial times, are the most prone to this fervent justification. Wanting their children to have a better life than they have becomes their rallying cry. A child's success reflects well on these parents, sanctifying the sacrifices they have made. Others drive home the need to excel so that their hard-won level of status is not diminished by a child's life that is less successful than their own. None of these reasons are bad in and of themselves. However, the unintentional ramifications of instilling this drive to stand out can have detrimental side effects. There is a fundamental distinction between *being the best* and *doing your best* and if that profound, yet delicate, difference becomes blurred, the result is a confusing ethos for life.

When the mandate to *being the best*, as opposed to *doing your best*, crosses the threshold of self-enrichment and personal fulfillment, and becomes an obsession, then pride can become the object of desire. The aspiration to transcend becomes an all-out competition, both inwardly and outwardly, and anything short of winning translates into one believing they are plain or average. The self-induced belief that one is not special can invoke the misguided feeling that how one views himself is how others see them. This can be emotionally intolerable and the joy of life can be diminished in direct proportion to the level of one's belief they are simply average. Therefore, their lives can become a quest against normalcy, a never-ending marathon of pursuing accomplishments intended to overcome their fear of not being special. Moreover, as they continue through life, sometimes casting aside the intrinsic, moral underpinnings they believe are slowing them down, they can ultimately miss seeing and experiencing the very things that would make their lives special. This is not to say that all forms of pride are bad. Pride in workmanship manifests itself in quality products and services, as well as a level of excellence that brings us stunningly beautiful photographs, enduring artwork, timeless architecture, and memorable music.

There are those blessed with being content with who they are and with their lot in life. Whether this perspective of themselves and their lives is the result of their upbringing, their education, their native culture, their faith, or simply a conscious choice, there is one thing they

> ### Native American Wisdom
>
> *"Furthermore, it was the rule of our life to share the fruits of our skill and success with our less fortunate brothers and sisters. Thus we kept our spirits free from the clog of pride, avarice or envy, and carried out, as we believed, the divine decree—a matter profoundly important to us."* [39] - Charles Alexander Eastman, Ohiyesa (Dakota Sioux)

generally all have in common—humility and humbleness. With that humility there is generally a level of happiness that frees them to succeed in the areas that eternally matter: relationships with families, friends, and God. Thankfully, that humility is often passed like a torch to their children and can be the key to their contentment, as well.

Mom and I both grew up with some of the conditions mentioned earlier. As the first-born, we were expected to excel and for most of our lives we did not see, nor experience, any of the downsides to working to be the best. Frankly, being the best when it was within our power to be so was quite rewarding. It built character and taught us to overcome formidable challenges—lessons that have served us well all through our lives. Black belts, championship trophies, recognition plaques, award certificates and degrees adorn our walls and bookcases. Our parents were so proud and they still are—and so are we.

At least for me though, despite the multitude of successes I have garnered in my life, there was a sinister side to all this success brewing below the surface. It was not until after two failed marriages that this flaw in the never-ending quest for excellence came to light. Being the best had become a foundational goal for my self-worth—not merely an outward representation of my abilities, passions and drive. Winning had become paramount. However, like a junkie constantly needing a fix, the ecstasy of winning became more and more short-lived and I needed more and more in order to maintain a positive outlook on my worth. I do not know if a loss of humility was ever a causality of my pursuits against normalcy but being humble in defeat never came easily. It was not until our A.T. adventure that I came to realize the fruitlessness of my preoccupation with being *the best* and learned how I could be satisfied with *doing my best*. The line between the two is still dangerously thin, and there are times when it is obscured altogether. However, now I can recognize it and not let my excursions across it undermine my happiness.

We planned and trained for our A.T. thru-hike for five years—trying out different types of equipment, taking numerous multi-day training hikes, and working out the minutest of details. We adopted the motto of *"Quitting is not an option"* and were certain that the infamous Appalachian Trail would fall a hapless victim to the honing of our abilities and the power of our will. In a sense, it was a competition, us against the trail, and we were certain we would prevail. On March 25, 2006 we left the Len Foote Hike Inn, walked up the access trail to Springer Mountain, and took our first steps on the A.T.

On day three, we left the Slaughter Creek Tentsite and headed up Blood Mountain, a beast of a mountain that challenged every ounce of physical training we had endured while getting prepared for our adventure. It was the first of many times when we came to understand the meaning of humility.

*March 28th:*

> *"Last evening brought with it a March cold that wrapped its bitter arms around both the mountain and our campsite like an angry grey ghost. It was fortunate that we had our winter bags or we would have suffered through a very uncomfortable night—and it was way too early in our journey to have faced that. We awoke to the patter of sleet spitting on our tent so we packed up quickly and headed to the dry security of Blood Mountain Shelter to eat our breakfast. It was a grueling climb, a savage initiation into the "thru-hiking" fraternity." Our legs and knees already ached, our Achilles burned and, had it not been for the frequent stops to take photographs of our surroundings, we would have questioned our ability to even make it to the Walasi-Yi Hostel on the other side of the mountain. It was frustrating and demoralizing to be struggling this much this soon on our hike.*
>
> *At the top sat the Blood Mountain Shelter, a bedraggled rock shelter that has been standing guard over the summit of*

*this mountain for decades. It was welcome and spectacular, almost as spectacular as the views from the overlooks near its front door. As invulnerable to the elements as its thick stone walls appeared, the dark cavern of the shelter was no match for the damp, cold air that wandered in and out of the front door, so we quickly ate our breakfast and headed back out on the trail.*

*As if the walk up this mountain had not already undermined our belief in our physical prowess, the trip down was even more daunting. Though we took our time, seeing that it was going to be a short day, each steep, brutal step jarred our knees and our confidence. By the time we reached the bottom, we were more than a bit demoralized. We had done preparation hikes in Colorado and on Camels Hump, in Vermont, to prepare for such a difficult ascent and descent and we were glad we did. That being said, there was still an undercurrent of disappointment running through our souls because it had been a harder hike than we were willing to admit—and that went against the grain of our "be the best" natures."* – Windtalker & Mom

The trail's penchant for confronting our egos and devastating any pride we took in our hiking ability, ability that we believed to be as good as anyone else's on the trail, would be a constant source of frustration for us. This day on Blood Mountain was only the first of many days when we would have to deal with the emotional upheaval of not meeting our own expectations. The next six months would be a constant lesson in humility that we were not sure we were comfortable with. If trying to *beat the trail* was not enough of a challenge to our pride and prowess, we also unexpectedly found ourselves comparing our efforts to those of our hiking companions and not only pride, but also its equally ugly twin, jealousy, raised its head to define our days.

*"If you start thinking to yourselves, "I did all this; and all by myself. I'm rich. It's all mine!"—well, think again. Remember that God, your God, gave you the strength to produce all this wealth so as to confirm the covenant that he promised to your ancestors—as it is today."* – Deuteronomy 8:17-18 (The Message)

We jokingly, though not at first, called them "the gazelles." They were the multitude of twenty-something college graduates that flooded the trail. Most were on a quest to use six months of unbridled freedom in which to sort through their options for the future, or to postpone as long as possible taking on the responsibilities required of a working adult. It was not their youthful exuberance, or their propensity for making their thru-hike as much of a social event as it was a life-changing adventure, that eventually stuck in our craw. It was the fact that they all seemed to be six-feet tall, most of which was legs, so they could hike much faster than we could. They were so fast that they often slept until eight or nine o'clock in the morning and still made it to their destination before dark. We generally were out of camp by 7:00 a.m. because it took us until dark to cover the same number of miles they did. To make matters worse, they usually arrived at the shelter or campsite hours before us, having flown by while we ate lunch. Equally frustrating was listening to them bantering back and forth about how many miles they covered in a day—oftentimes twenty or more. It often took us twelve hours to cover just fifteen miles.

We decided near the start of our hike that Mom would lead. Though her pace was a bit slower than mine was, it was a mutual decision made so that she had better views of the trail ahead—views that would minimize her taking a fall. However, every time a gazelle flew by us, it was a decision that I woefully regretted. I viewed being passed as an affront to my pride and skill and it negatively altered my demeanor, putting me in the foulest of moods. I am not proud to say that I often vocalized my displeasure with our pace but my comments did nothing to make us go faster—it merely exacerbated the situation. Mom was initially discouraged by being passed as well, but she kept it to herself and more readily accepted that this was the way it was going to be all the way to Maine. It was not until a month or two later, after my pride had been repeatedly crushed, that I accepted the fact that we were never going to be the first ones into camp. To counteract the feelings of inadequacy brought about by our acceptance of being slower than virtually everyone else was, we humorously dubbed ourselves "the gerbils." We began to relish being slow because it gave us the opportunity to experience elements of our journey we would have missed simply focusing on beating everyone else. As the saying goes, *"It's not about the destination, it is about the journey."*

At times, being proud and wanting to beat the gazelles to camp, became so all encompassing that it threatened the pleasure of the journey. Pride undermined our enjoyment of each other, and had we not been careful, our disdain for *the winners* could have easily infiltrated our conversations with them, creating a barrier to our relationships. All they were doing was hiking at a pace that was comfortable for them—they did not hike fast to beat us to camp or to make us miserable. That was our problem. We had inadvertently made our hike a contest, an accomplishment we could check off our life lists. Once we came to grips with the fact that our pride over this truly insignificant aspect of our trip was negatively affecting our excitement, things began to change dramatically. Our only wish was that we could have learned this lesson sooner, for we fear we overlooked some of the trail's beauty during the early stages of our hike.

Living humbly was a lesson that we needed to constantly be reminded of. Through our insistence on trying to hike faster than the gazelles and repeatedly failing, our prideful spirits were exposed every day. Once we accepted the fact that we would be miserable until we let go of our competitive natures, we also came to realize that our pride often gets in the way of our relationship with God, our friends, family and co-workers, as well. We began living each day in the moment. A moment-by-moment approach to the hike was refreshing. Now that we are home and the specter of being the best still regularly attempts to rear its ugly head, we reflect on the lessons in humility we learned on the trail to remind us of how much more pleasant and rewarding being humble can be. Overcoming a prideful spirit is a process—one that opens up the door to a better understanding and appreciation of a relationship with God. It is learning experience in which we need to put our egos aside in order to thoroughly enjoy the riches of the journey—and life.

> *"......All of you, clothe yourselves with humility toward one another, because, 'God opposes the proud but gives grace to the humble.' Humble yourselves, therefore, under God's mighty hand, that he may lift you up in due time."* - 1 Peter 5:5-6

Life on the Appalachian Trail is akin to real life in so many ways— with many of the same challenges, pitfalls and rewards. In life, as on the trail, a vain and overconfident attitude can result in disastrous consequences. Competing with the other hikers, if only in the privacy of your own mind to see who is the fastest or who can hike the most miles per day, is not the only prideful challenge to be overcome. After hiking hundreds and hundreds of miles, it is easy to become a bit "cocky" about your ability. Even still, there is always a nagging fear in the back of your mind that a moment of carelessness could cause you to be injured, thus ending your journey. By midway in your journey, you have developed into a lean, mean hiking machine, impervious to only the most flagrant lapses in judgment, but this is when you become the most vulnerable. As you near the end of the A.T., it is easy to become full of yourself and that is usually when the trail humbles you.

*"With less than 200 miles to go, the inevitable finally happened. After 1,980.6 miles of flawless hiking, I finally fell. In my mind, I had established a personal goal for myself—one that would set my hike apart from everyone else's. That goal was to complete the entire A.T. without once falling. Now my goal, as well as my ego, was shattered and my perfect hike was marred. The actual fall was nothing major, compared to the amount of distress it caused me to wrestle with. I just tried to climb up the face of a medium-size rock with a muddy boot and slipped, giving my knee quite a shot. Though personally aggravated by my loss of balance, Mom was glad I finally took a tumble. Since I had not yet fallen, like virtually everyone else on the trail, she had become increasingly concerned that when I did fall, it would be a fall of monumental proportions. Now she felt she could rest a bit easier. However, with my streak broken, the wheels were set in motion for more episodes of clumsiness.*

*Not long after my rock mishap, I found myself sitting in the waters of Long Pond Stream, pack and all, floundering like a beached whale as I tried to get up. I attempted to rock-hop across, unconsciously took a wrong step, and slipped on a rock hidden beneath some gentle rapids. Down I went, spewing out a list of demonstrably un-Christian expletives that immediately had me asking the Creator for forgiveness. Luckily, my pride took more of a beating than either my body or my gear. I looked upstream to where my bride had successfully forded—and had her camera in hand—to see a rather large grin spread across her face. To mitigate the embarrassment of my less-than-graceful dive into the water, I forced a smile onto my own face.*

*Believing my run of bad luck had ended, I was once again snatched back to the reality of the trail as we left the site of trail magic near Nahmakanta Lake in Maine. Somehow, as* we waltzed through a rather placid section of trail, I managed to locate the only branch on the ground, got it caught between both of my feet, and did a swan dive into the pine needles that covered the trail. By now, my ego could take no more and I was beside myself. Mom on the other hand, giggled again—though only after she was sure I was all right.

It was now September 22$^{nd}$ and we had made it 2,156 miles—only a measly 18.6 miles left to go. We were almost there and the excitement of being so close to Mt. Katahdin put a lilt in our step that we had not had for some time. Only one more day and we would stand at the foot of the holy grail of thru-hiking, 'The Greatest Mountain,'—'Le Grande K.' It was an incredible day in every way, except for one potentially disastrous event.

It was the first day of fall and in retrospect that turned out to be ironic. Late in the afternoon, we neared the Hurd Brook Lean-To where we would undoubtedly rendezvous, possibly for the last time, with a large contingent of our trail family. We approached a bend in the trail blocked by a large oak tree lying across it. Trail maintainers had yet to remove it from the path, and because it was so large, there was no visible way for us to go around it. It was suspended several feet in the air like a giant, black, foreboding monster. Mom boosted herself up onto the top of it, swung her legs over the opposite side, and then dropped to the pile of rocks on the trail below. She accomplished this series of moves with such ease I did not give this barricade the respect it deserved. Taking "Mom's" route, I used the exact same approach to get over the tree. There was one big difference, though. When I swung my legs over and dropped down, I attempted to come down on just my right foot. Being overconfident, and disregarding the requisite care necessary for such a task, I looked up at "Mom," rather than at my feet and severely miscalculated the distance to the rocks below. I suddenly, and disastrously, found myself free falling, completely missing the resting place for my right foot. I came crashing down on the rocks on my right thigh with the full force of both my falling body and pack. "Burner's" prophetic statement, several days earlier, about him getting hurt so close to the end of the hike, immediately flashed through my mind.

114

*'Oh, my God!' I heard Mom scream, before my pain even started to settle in.*

*She had turned around to make sure I made it over successfully and had viewed the entire, gut-wrenching, event. As she raced back toward me, the pain began to race through my body like a surge of high-voltage electricity. It was the type of pain that instantaneously drained the blood from my head and turned my face as chalky white as the clouds overhead. It caused my stomach to convulse, making me want to vomit. As I writhed on the ground, clutching my thigh in the most intense pain I had felt since I broke my foot in a wildly flipping go-kart many years earlier, Mom stripped my pack from my back. Sensing I was beginning to hyperventilate to counteract the pain, she placed her calming hand on my forehead. In a motherly tone of voice, while resting my head in her lap, she urged me to relax and take slow, deep breaths.*

*I lay on the ground for quite some time as the initial pain subsided and Mom suggested I pull down my pants so she could view the damage. When I had hit the pile of rocks we had both heard a mind-numbing, cracking sound and her fear was that I had broken my leg. A break so high up on my femur would surely put an end to our journey. There was no visible sign of a break, no piercing of the skin, and that was a good sign. However, the pain was intense enough to indicate a possible internal break. I was not sure if it was the lingering pain or the thought of having to end our hike that caused my eyes to tear up.*

*Then, thinking back to the courage she exhibited after her fall just before Stratton Pond, my own sense of determination took hold. There was no way, after all we had been through, that I was going to let my partner down—broken leg or no broken leg. This was not going to be an impediment to us moving forward and finishing what we started. Placing my hand on her shoulder for support, I stood up and put weight on my throbbing leg. The pain was excruciating, but the leg did not give way. Thank God! I hobbled around for a few minutes, giving it a thorough test and then turned to my best friend, whose face still had grave concern written all over it.*

*'Let's go! I need to walk this off!' I insisted through clenched teeth.*

*Since my pace would now be measurably slower than usual, Mom insisted I lead the rest of the day so we could walk at a speed comfortable for me. In due time, the endorphins kicked in and I was back up to a pace that had Mom racing to keep up. As we entered the campground at Hurd Brook Lean-To, I was feeling much better but was well aware that I was going to have an extremely sore leg the rest of the hike. What was truly amazing was that despite the effects of the fall, we did one of our biggest mileage days in only eleven hours. I guess this was an example of what "Old Drum" called the "crazy drive of the thru-hikers." Evidently, the cracking sound we had both heard, that appeared to be a bone breaking, was the sound of my trekking poles hitting the rocks beneath me.*

*Vitamin "I," Ibuprofen, would be my staple food for the next several days and I eventually ended up with a leg that was every conceivable color of yellow, blue, and purple one could imagine—from my ankle to my thigh."* – Windtalker & Mom

All of these falls, especially the last one, which in hindsight was the culmination of my not learning my lesson in humility from my previous minor falls, provided valuable insight into the ramifications of being full of myself. Not only did I now have the physical reminder of my futile desire to be better than everyone else by never falling, but now my pride and over-confident nature had been reduced to emotional rubble.

*"Pride goes before destruction, a haughty spirit before a fall."*
– Proverbs 16:18 (NIV)

Life presents its own share of falls, especially when we pursue it with an egotistical heart. Our lives can become a competition, a self-centered race to "make it" and join the ranks of the adored and revered. Satisfaction in simply being who we are created to be just does not seem to suffice. Satisfaction in achieving God's plan for us, the plan that He so lovingly and painstakingly put together, takes a backseat to our striving to meet society's, and our own, definition of achievement and worth. On the surface, striving can reap some remarkable rewards. But, there is also a dark side to the quest for notoriety and self-fulfillment. Even though we are constantly reminded of this fact in news stories of celebrities' and politicians' falls from grace, we still reach for the brass ring, whatever it might be. Maybe we do this because the rewards of these self-seeking pursuits of greatness are tangible and visible—we can read about them, hear about them on the news and entertainment channels, and some become the subjects of hit movies. God's plan for us is seldom that evident, and despite all the signs we are given, what He has for us is often still a mystery, one we are incapable of seeing or understanding without His help. Interestingly enough, because we are often unable to grasp the concept of how much more rewarding God's plan is for our lives, He has ways of getting our attention simply by allowing us to experience the futility of <u>our</u> own plans.

> *"I'll break your strong pride: I'll make the skies above you like a sheet of tin and the ground under you like cast iron. No matter how hard you work, nothing will come of it: No crops out of the ground, no fruit off the trees."* - Leviticus 26:19
> (The Message)

I met Kelly Minter quite a number of years ago when she was a fledgling Christian singer/songwriter and was the opening act at a concert I was producing. We kept in contact over the years and I was blessed by being able to run sound for her at one of her concerts and to work with her at an Academy of Gospel Music Association event in Virginia. After years of toiling in the Christian music scene, she wrote a book entitled, *Water into Wine – Hope for the Miraculous in the Struggle of the Mundane,* in which she recounts her quest for greatness and the realizations that came about because of it.

> *"I had just moved to Nashville, begun my first bus tour and released a record—all within the span of a week. I might as well have gotten married for good measure—it seemed like the perfect time to throw in one more life-changing event. My record company had secured me an "opportunity" (code for something that is undesirable, seemingly optional, but really mandatory) with a company that was web streaming the Dove Awards from backstage. The Doves are to contemporary Christian music what the Grammys are to secular music. As*

*the award winners were whisked offstage and into the publicity room, my job was to type their interview questions and answers, real time, for the online world to follow."* [40]

This hardly seemed like the job for someone who had *obviously* made it in the music world, even though it had only been for a week. But, as her record company assured her, the visibility would be good for her and her exposure to other, more well-known artists, could reap huge benefits for her career. She goes on to say this was not how she imagined her first appearance at the Dove Awards but she was confident that her record company was giving her this opportunity to get exposure as new artist. As she stated,

*"Whatever it took to get me where I wanted to go."* [41]

She then continued.

*"I was just beginning to get the hang of the evening when one of the best and brightest artists from the label I had just signed with came through the door. Although we had met on a few occasions and had even hung out at some industry functions together, nothing about me seemed to be ringing a bell for him. As he stepped up to the table, he reached out his hand and asked me how long I had been working as an interviewer. Too embarrassed to remind him that I was a labelmate and <u>not</u> a professional interviewer, I sheepishly responded, 'Not long.' As in, like, the last thirty minutes. To deepen my humiliation, a woman from his entourage later tugged on my arm and asked if I could get her a Diet Coke. 'Uhhh, sure...No problem.' What am I doing here?*

*The evening ended as disappointingly as it started. I left feeling like an outsider, as if the whole event was for people who had somehow figured out how to crack the code of superiority for which I had yet to discover the code."* [42]

She has had her own set of accomplishments over the years, but finally came to realize the futility and emptiness of a life built on pursuing the glitz and glamour of being famous. She readily admits that she now just smiles and feels relieved that that part of her life is over—that she is no longer controlled by the need to be renowned or to compare her life to anyone else's.

*"Seeing the hordes of people lining up for an opportunity to get a mere glimpse of them, I thought that their level of prestige was well worth whatever struggle it would take to get there myself. My thinking was logical but amiss: 'If everyone is after them, they must have something I lack—something I need in order to be okay.'"* [43]

We are all God's creations, part of the magnificent universe that to this day, despite all the advances in science and technology, still mystifies us with its beauty and complexity. Who are we, just tiny grains of sand in His eternal plan that we believe we can survive and prosper through our own strength and cunning? We have not been put on earth to find our self-esteem in winning. Instead, God offers us self-worth through His love and acceptance of who we are.

God gave Mom and me the opportunity, health and resources to pursue a dream unlike any other we had ever had. He had laid out before us the beauty of the wilderness for us to wander through and as we wandered we eventually learned much about ourselves, the good and the bad, just as He had planned. We also learned about the rewards that came from moving our egos aside and letting His presence fill the void. Once our pride and sense of accomplishment were no longer the driving forces behind our journey, we were free to experience more fully, feel more deeply and understand more clearly, who He is, who we are, and who He wanted us to become. As we triumphantly stood high atop Mt. Katahdin, yes, we were proud of our accomplishment. However, that pride was tempered by a new feeling of humility, a humility born from our understanding that we could not have done it without His grace and protection each day.

*"I look up at your macro-skies, dark and enormous,*
*your handmade sky-jewelry,*
*Moon and stars mounted in their settings.*
*Then I look at my micro-self and wonder,*
*Why do you bother with us?*
*Why take a second look our way?"* - Psalm 8: 3-4
(The Message)

Such should be the way we approach life. How could we possibly be smarter and know more about what will truly satisfy us than the One who created us, and everything around us? Of course, He wants us to succeed magnificently, for our success is a testament to His

119

influence in our lives. God is no different from any other proud father when his children succeed—and succeed because those children heeded the advice and counsel he gave to them. Moreover, when those children erase their pride and give credit for their success to their father—that is the meaning of true success.

*"Make sure you don't forget God, your God, by not keeping his commandments, his rules and regulations that I command you today. Make sure that when you eat and are satisfied, build pleasant houses and settle in, see your herds and flocks flourish and more and more money come in, watch your standard of living going up and up—make sure you don't become so full of yourself and your things that you forget God, your God..."* – Deuteronomy 8:11-14 (The Message)

---

## Devotional: *"Humility"*

*"Pride goes before destruction, a haughty spirit before a fall".* - Proverbs 16:18

Pride can have good connotations, as in a job well done. However, when defined as the opposite of humility, it also means arrogance, conceit, haughtiness, egotism, and self-centeredness. I have a hard time balancing between my expectations of excellence and perfection. This is especially hard if you've lived your whole life seeking to be the best, or do the best, or trying to live up to your own or other's high expectations. I know that perfection is not possible in this life. But, I still think about striving for excellence in everything I do. The trail was a reminder that my "excellence" at speed and miles per day were not the best (in fact, we felt like we were the slowest people out there) and it was frustrating and even embarrassing. This aspect of our trail experience was an awakening that sometimes I think I needed to "take me down a peg!"

At this moment, I think my struggle with humility has to do with playing a comparison game, competing and judging myself against others. I need to find a way to feel good about myself—about doing the best possible job with the skills, gifts, and abilities God has given to me, without comparing results to someone else. I need a way to remind myself that I haven't done it all on my own, that it's not all about me, and that life is really not a competition. Going back to the definition, the concept of self-centered comes into play when I describe my struggle.

I have to say, while we had so many daily lessons on humility on the trail, it is remains an issue that continues to haunt me. I fear that humility is going to be something I struggle with my entire life. When will I understand that it's really not about me? – *Mom*

## Prayer

*"God, you created us with drive, determination, perseverance and the desire to do the best with what you have given us. Yet, you also created us with a need to be humble before you and one another. We can only find the right balance with your help! Help me learn to be other-centered."*

# The Walk

*"Success has nothing to do with what you gain in life or accomplish for yourself. It's what you do for others." –*
Danny Thomas

When Benton MacKaye, a regional planner, came up with the concept of the Appalachian Trail in 1921, it was to be part of a long-range plan to lure people from the urban centers of the east coast to an easily accessible wilderness sanctuary, free of noise, cars and confusion. It was to be a place where people could relax and revel in the natural surroundings, while satisfying their souls' need to escape and rejuvenate itself. And so it began, and in 1937, through the cooperation of private clubs, government agencies, and the leadership of Myron Avery, who was elected president of The Potomac Appalachian Trail Club in 1927, a post he held until 1940, MacKaye's concept became a reality.

It stands today as the country's second oldest long-distance hiking trail and the first completed national scenic trail—a designation it received in 1968—and is a privately managed unit of the National Park System. It is the nation's longest marked footpath, at just under 2,200 miles, and crosses six other units of the National Park System, traverses eight national forests, and passes through fourteen states. It also crosses numerous state and local parks.

Estimates are that over half of the country's population lives within a day's drive of the A.T., making it the most accessible and most used trail in the country. More than ten-thousand people have reported hiking the length of the trail—some in sections, over a number of years, and some as thru-hikes, hiking from Georgia to Maine, or Maine to Georgia, in one continuous hike, a hike comprised of an estimated five-million footsteps.

As incredible as all these statistics about the trail may be, the one that stands out above all the rest is that the A.T. is maintained by more than six-thousand volunteers, in thirty separate trail clubs, who contribute in excess of 200,000 hours each year to keep the trail open and in excellent shape. Under the lead organization for the trail, the

Appalachian Trail Conservancy, in cooperation with the trail clubs, National Park Service, state parks, and other governmental agencies, the effort to protect and maintain this trail is the largest volunteer/government cooperative effort in the world. The efforts of these volunteers are truly amazing. As one walks the thousands of miles of rock, root and dirt treadway that makes up the Appalachian Trail, it is seldom that one ever takes for granted their hard work and dedication. The A.T. is a shining example of volunteerism at its best— people giving back to "the trail"—and they do it with no desire for personal gain or public recognition. They do it simply because they love the trail and see it as their responsibility to care for it and protect it. In doing so, they also care for and protect the hikers. It is their passion.

> ### Native American Wisdom
> *"No person among us desires any other reward for performing a brave and worthy action, but the consciousness of having served his nation."* [44] - Joseph Brant, Thayendanegea (Mohawk)

Aside from the positive affect that being on the trail had on our level of stress, our ability to be flexible and adapt to changing situations, our capacity to build relationships, and our overall sense of wonder over the sights, sounds and smell of the wilderness, there was one unexpected side effect. The longer we were wonderfully held in the surreal embrace of nature, the more we felt compelled to volunteer in some way after we had accomplished our goal of reaching Mt. Katahdin. Considering all that the trail had given us, how it had enriched our lives and our relationship with each other, it seemed only fitting that we give something back. Oddly, this decision to volunteer never felt like we were fulfilling any sort of obligation or mandate—it just seemed like the right and natural thing to do. It simply remained to be seen in which arena we would apply our newly found passion. Would it be as trail angels or trail maintainers? Maybe there would be some other way, that best used our gifts and talents, which would be of greater value to those who used the trail. Our feelings were not uncommon among other thru-hikers, many of whom also felt the burning desire to keep the memory of their time on the A.T. alive through service.

One of the people we know who was influenced by his journey to give back something is an orthopedic physician's assistant named Ken Berry—better known during his 2006 thru-hike as "Bone Pac."

Because he began his hike in late February, a full month before us, we never had the pleasure of meeting him on the trail. However, we read his entries in the shelter registers and heard some of the amazing trail stories about him.

In August of 2006, only two months after completing his hike, Bone Pac began the process of giving back to the trail in the way he had chosen. He would open a hostel. He and his wife, Jennel, bought a home right near the trail in Smithsburg, Maryland. It was large enough to hold both their growing family and the type of hostel Ken envisioned. The first floor of the house is where Ken and his family would live. Up a short flight of steps, is the second floor and this was converted into the hostel, complete with a carpeted bunk room, showers, a laundry

> ### Native American Wisdom
> *"The public position of the Indian has always been entirely dependent upon our private virtue. We are never permitted to forget that we do not live to ourselves alone, but to our tribe and clan. Every child, from the first days of learning, is a public servant in training."* [45] - Charles Alexander Eastman, Ohiyesa (Dakota Sioux)

room, heat and air conditioning, internet service, and an area to simply relax. Since the hostel is only a short drive from our home, we visited the Free State Hostel after its opening in 2007 and got to meet Ken and his family. What we saw in his eyes and heard in his voice when he talked about the hostel, was clear evidence of the effect the trail had on him and on his life. The hostel was not only a demonstration of his love for hikers and the trail, but also a manifestation of his love for God and his desire to serve. http://www.freestatehiker.com

> *"For we are God's workmanship, created in Christ Jesus to do good works, which God prepared in advance for us to do."* – Ephesians 2:10 (NIV)

Craig and Suzy Miles, a.k.a. "Clay and Branch," who we had the good fortune of hiking with for a few days early in our thru-hike, found their own special way to give back. Though they were never able to complete their full thru-hike due to injuries, their undeniable and unyielding faith became the foundation for their mission.

> *"Do not merely listen to the word, and so deceive yourselves. Do what it says. Anyone who listens to the word but does not do what it says is like a man who looks at his face in a mirror and, after looking at himself, goes away and immediately*

*forgets what he looks like. But the man who looks intently into the perfect law that gives freedom, and continues to do this, not forgetting what he has heard, but doing it—he will be blessed in what he does."* – James 1:22-25 (NIV)

They began the Appalachian Trail Servants Ministry, www.trailministry.org, offering love, compassion, and faith-based outreach to hikers all along the A.T. They accepted the challenge issued to all Christians by James and are living out their faith through works.

*"On the trail, there are physical, emotional, and even spiritual challenges. The physical challenge is obvious. Blisters and muscle soreness often weed out about 20 percent of the hikers in the first 30.7 miles at Neels Gap, GA. arguably, after this point, the emotional challenge begins. As one continues North on the A.T., the emotional challenge may transform into a spiritual challenge for some. Generally, thru-hikers are spiritually-minded people. However, while many thru-hikers believe in God via general revelation through nature, unfortunately, most thru-hikers do not believe in God's special revelation-Jesus Christ. Instead, these hikers view religion and theology as being deeply personal. Because of this view, many people on the A.T. also believe that the church is irrelevant to their lives. One person that we polled even stated that the woods are his "cathedral."*

*Although many hikers are searching for something more in life, some hikers are hostile to anyone who might infringe upon their personal spirituality. Sadly, after hiking 2,175 miles, many thru-hikers are left feeling empty. For these hikers, the goal of finishing the A.T. may have been met but they lack purpose in life. So, they hike the trail again and again. In fact, one fellow that we polled has hiked 17,000 miles thus far in his quest to find 'something more' in life! Moreover, in our polling, we found that many thru-hikers suffer from post-hike depression and some hikers encounter difficulty fitting back into society. Therefore, it is our purpose to serve the physical, emotional, and spiritual needs of these hikers. By doing this, we hope that hikers will take the next step toward Christ and gain a purpose in life. Appalachian*

*Trail Servants will achieve this goal in two ways—through Trail Angels and Trail Chaplains."* [46] - Clay & Branch

Clay and Branch are not alone in their mission and enlist "Trail Chaplains," like Brett and Bronwyn Stamps, a.k.a. "Social" and "Dandelion," to help carry out their ministry. In 2006, the same year we completed our thru-hike, "Social" and "Dandelion" successfully completed their journey to the glory of the Lord. Unfortunately, they were about a week behind us so we never met them, but from reading their journals, it is obvious they had a positive effect on everyone they did meet.

*"Words really can not describe our experience on the Appalachian Trail. We would do it again in a heartbeat. Spiritually, you experience God's Greatness as well as the simplicity of being a Christian. We learned to sit back and just be in awe of our Creator. From the incredible views to getting us to a shelter before the rains came, His hand was everywhere! While hiking, we would spend quite a bit of time in prayer. Sometimes it was for help getting up the mountain in front of us and other times it was for the people we were hiking with. Friendships formed on the trail pretty quickly as we were all going through the same ups and downs (literally). Many hikers opened up quickly and we realized they were really searching for something. Fortunately, we knew what that something was and were able to share our relationship with Christ with them—not just verbally but through our every day actions. It is amazing looking back at our pictures and seeing the hiking group that God put together for us, some Christians some not. The large majority of the people we started really hiking with in the Smokies finished with us at Katahdin! Over that many miles, it was truly a God thing! We are still in touch with many of them and plan to continue to plant seeds and pray for those who do not know Christ.*

*A fellow Christian hiker at the top of Katahdin said 'If all Christians treated each other the way thru-hikers treat each other, wouldn't it be wonderful?' It's true, no one judged you for the way you looked or smelled or dressed and everyone would go out of their way to help if someone was hurt, needed laundry done, wanted something from the store, or even needed money. Although our miles ended at Katahdin our mission did not. We thank God for the opportunity for such an amazing journey!"* [47] - Social & Dandelion

Other thru-hikers did not wait until their hike was over to serve others. Many had a specific mission and vision for their pilgrimage, a way to serve as they made their way from Georgia to Maine. Years ago, Jeff Alt, a.k.a. "Wrong Foot," thru-hiked the A.T. in order to raise money for the Sunshine Home. Sunshine Home is a facility where his brother Aaron, who suffers from cerebral palsy and mental retardation, lives. There were days during our hike when we trudged along with "Model T" who was raising funds with his hike so the Salvation Army in his hometown could build a shelter and "Old Drum" was raising money for a college scholarship program at his alma mater. Then there was "Tyvek," a Vietnam veteran, who hiked the A.T. barefoot, to bring more awareness to the ongoing problem of soldiers who suffer from post-traumatic stress disorder and to raise money for counseling programs to help veterans returning from war.

Not everyone having a passion for service was actually hiking—many, be they people of faith or not, were along the roadsides and in the towns through which the A.T. passed. Their sole mission was to serve the hikers themselves; for example, Jeff Patrick, at Mt Rogers Outfitters in Damascus, Virginia, who provides a comfortable hostel and shuttles to-and-from the trail and the monks at the Graymoor Spiritual Life Center in New York, who model spiritual strength and provide a place for weary hikers to stay. And then there are the legions of trail angels—those who appear when you least expect them, to share their love of the trail, and the hikers, by serving up food and beverages, providing shuttles into town, and always offering greatly needed, and much appreciated, encouragement. No two people exemplified the heart of the trail angel more than did V&A who drove their RV the entire length of the A.T. providing, not only trail support to us, but seeing to the needs of so many of the thru-hikers that crossed their path. The joy they discovered in giving has stayed with them ever since. For many of these wonderful and endearing people, this outpouring of compassion is an obvious act of faith. For the others, if it is not, their actions certainly exemplify such a life-style.

It was not until our adventure was over that we discovered how we could best use our gifts, talents and passions to give back to the trail. Our affection for the A.T. was a given, and since we were both gifted with an ability for public speaking and possessed the talents to put together multi-media presentations, we decided to give talks about our hike. Through these presentations, we devote ourselves to informing people about the A.T. and motivating them to consider attempting what we accomplished. Over the course of a few years, we developed numerous talks targeted at potential long-distance hikers, as well as for those who prefer shorter hikes. *Windtalker & Mom's Appalachian Trail Thru-Hike,* provides an overview of the trail and the specifics of our hike. *The Care & Feeding of the Long-Distance Hiker* focuses on the physical hurdles of a long-distance hike and how to overcome them. For couples who are considering hiking together, we developed, *The Joys of Backpacking as a Couple,* which explains the unique challenges and rewards we, and others, experienced hiking as a couple. *Spiritual Reflections from the Appalachian Trail,* revolves around the juxtaposition of a thru-hike and a walk of faith, and forms the basis for this book. *Dream It! Plan It! Live It!* is a motivational presentation that uses our thru-hike as a backdrop to inspire people to pursue their dreams, no matter what their age.

We are fortunate to have the opportunities to pass on our knowledge and passion at numerous venues such as the Damascus Appalachian Trail Days, The Rutland Long Trail Festival, Greenbrier State Park in Maryland, Shenandoah National Park, REI stores, Boy Scout troops, Rotary Clubs, for professional organizations, and at various churches. We both became "Trail Talkers" for the Potomac Appalachian Trail Club, telling people about hiking and trails at community events, and I eventually became Supervisor of Activities for the PATC. Our greatest joy, however, is providing trail magic as often as we can.

> *"In the same way, let your light shine before men, that they may see your good deeds and praise your Father in heaven."*
> – Mathew 5:16 (NIV)

Our desire to give back in this way was not something that we had to summon up from the deep recesses of our souls. It was bred from the trail culture that we were a part of each day—a culture that exemplified love, compassion, security, encouragement and hope. Caring about each other in these ways, and serving each other, became so second-nature to all of us that it was akin to breathing in the fresh, crisp mountain air or taking the next step across a river. We did not think about it, we just selflessly did it, and the personal rewards are countless.

A life of faith is equally rewarding when pursued with the same unselfish desire to care for those around us. As children of God, we are called to do as much. There are trail angels, like "Goin' Home" and "Potato Man," who, at their own personal expense, provide several days of hearty meals and a place to pitch a tent for a day's rest. "Jeopardy" and "Java," also give of their time and resources to see that hikers have a good meal and place to rest, exemplify the Christian ethic of *"letting their light shine for all men."* Whether or not they are Christians, we do not know, but their actions

> ### Native American Wisdom
>
> *"Natives are very mindful of the fact that historically they have not had to be reminded to feed the hungry, clothe the poor or give shelter to those in need. For the most part they do it instinctively, sincerely and with pleasure. They visit the sick and afflicted and are sympathetic to those who suffer misfortune or disaster. Why? Because among Indian people, your neighbor is your relative. In this way the Native tradition is a strong portrait of the biblical reality of our oneness in Christ as the extended family of God—a true picture of the Body of Christ."* [48] - Richard Twiss, Taoyate Obnajin (Lakota/Sioux)

demonstrate the type of outreach those of faith offer to their communities—"absolutely free" love and compassion. Their acts were a constant reminder of what our lives as Christians should demonstrate.

If there is a single group of people, who stand out as the personification of selfless giving, it is the legion of trail maintainers who protect and care for trails everywhere. Yes, the thru-hikers receive the lion's share of the accolades and notoriety, but the unsung heroes of the trail, the people who are out there week in and week out, sometimes for 10, 20 and 30 years or more, are the trail maintainers. They are the *true heroes* of the A.T. Many have never thru-hiked the trail, but that fact has no bearing on the devotion they have to see that the A.T., and every other trail, are there for others to enjoy. What purer act of giving can there be? Their selfless commitment is a model of the Christian life—a life where each uses the gifts, talents, and passions given to them by God to do the work He has called them to do.

Mom and I are not gifted in trail maintenance and our passions do not lie in that area. However, through our presentations, using the gifts we have been uniquely given, we are able to give in the way we believe we are expected to. Using our gifts, we contribute to the whole of the trail experience—as the trail maintainers do with their gifts and passions. We are but one part of the "body" of the trail experience. So, how does using your special talents to give back to the trail pertain to a life of faith? What gifts and talents do you posses, and how can you best use them as part of *The Body of Christ?* If you have been party to the compassion, camaraderie and benevolence that is an integral part of A.T. life, then you already understand what a life of faith-filled service is all about. You simply need to take what you have learned on the trail and apply it to your daily Christian life.

> *"You are Christ's body—that's who you are! You must never forget this. Only as you accept your part of that body does your "part" mean anything. You're familiar with some of the parts that God has formed in his church, which is his "body": Apostles, prophets, teachers, miracle workers, healers, helpers, organizers, those who pray in tongues."* - 1
> Corinthians 12: 27-28 (The Message)

Virtually everyone is gifted at birth with special talents, as can be seen by the myriad of amazing artwork, architecture and technological advances around us. Equally astounding, yet often less visible, are the works of gifted teachers, leaders, doctors, scientists, entrepreneurs and those in the trades. The results of the application of their gifts contribute to the whole of society, making it the dynamic and interesting entity that it is. It is when those talents are used with a *spirit-filled* heart, and applied to bring others to a life of faith through walking the talk, that they truly become *spiritual gifts*. Musicians become worship leaders, teachers use their skills in Sunday school and in teaching God's word, tradesmen make free repairs on the home of a single mother struggling to get by, and athletes compete in special events to raise money for a worthwhile charity. What is most important is that serving is about <u>people</u>. Just like the Trail Days slogan, "People are the Trail," we should serve each other because "People are Life." No matter what your abilities, talents, or passions, as Christians we have all been created as part of the *body of Christ* and our contributions are important, unique, and eternal.

Christian songwriter, recording artist and writer, Kelly Minter, speaks of her original understanding of service—a perspective shared by many.

> *"The word "servanthood" is right up there with "obedience" in my list of topics I surreptitiously avoid. I have regularly*

*tensed up while listening to sermons or reading a book regarding this subject, squirming in my chair, desperately hoping I wouldn't actually be "convicted" to do something."* [49]

However, she goes on to explain that her aversion to *service* was predicated on what she saw as the narrow definition of service described by Christian culture. Someone who faithfully teaches Sunday school to first graders, cooks for the homeless, volunteers for various duties, or assumes someone else's unwanted chores epitomized this narrow view. Her attempts to be a "square peg in a round hole," and do "the servant thing," brought her nothing but annoyance, resentment and disappointment in herself. Then the true meaning of serving others came to light.

*"Over the past several years, I have been discovering a picture of servanthood that looks exceedingly different from what I once perceived. Turns out I've had it mostly wrong. Bottom line is that I had missed the very personal aspect of servanthood. I had fallen into the trap of serving the <u>system</u>, not a person. But servanthood by its very nature requires that <u>someone</u> be served, which is why it is personal. Servanthood is about people, and ultimately about God, because God desperately loves people. We err when we make it about principles or ideals."* [50]

Surely, not everyone who put their foot on that first white blaze atop Springer Mountain, with their eyes and heart focused on reaching Mt. Katahdin, brought to the trail the level of compassion and service to others that ultimately became a part of their daily lives on the trail. We are all human, after all. But, it was nearly impossible not to develop a love and sense of responsibility for your fellow man when each day you were offering, or receiving, as the bumper stickers say, "random acts of kindness."

Serving each other was a part of the trail culture, each person using his/her gifts and talents to help in any way they could. It was a cultural norm that exemplifies what God calls each of us to do in our daily lives. Despite the trials that we all faced, the cold, the heat, the rain, the pain and the bugs, there was always an overriding sense of pure joy in giving of ourselves that negated all those trials.

Often, in life, we feel dissatisfied despite all we <u>have</u>. However, in the final analysis, it comes down to how much we <u>give</u> to others that provides satisfaction. As famed writer Erma Bombeck puts it,

*"When I stand before God at the end of my life, I would hope that I would not have a single bit of talent left and could say, 'I used everything you gave me.'"*

---

# Devotional: *"Service"*

*"For we are God's workmanship, created in Christ Jesus to do good works, which God prepared in advance for us to do."* - Ephesians 2:10

The concept of service to our fellow man is not unique to Christianity. In fact, Albert Einstein wrote an essay called *"An Ideal of Service to Our Fellow Man"* in which he says that service to our fellow man is a moral and ethical matter that is not necessarily tied to our religion. His essay was part of a 1950's radio program called *"This I Believe"* in which Americans from all walks of life shared what they believed.

Well, this is what I believe about service. I believe God designed each of us to be unique, and that we are fearfully and wonderfully, made. Then, through our acceptance of Jesus' death on the cross, I believe we are called to serve with God to reach others to him. I have a passion for helping people identify their God-given SHAPE so that they can live with joy as God intended. SHAPE is an acronym for <u>S</u>piritual gifts, <u>H</u>eart (passion), <u>A</u>bilities, <u>P</u>ersonality, and <u>E</u>xperiences. Most often, this concept is used in Christian circles to describe the ways in which someone should serve others in ministry or missions. I believe that our service to others extends well beyond ministry in the church and includes every aspect of our lives and interactions with others.

Interestingly, the collection of trail clubs, trail maintainers, and government agencies along the Appalachian Trail is a collection of thousands of people, investing thousands upon thousands of hours every year, given to a single cause—the Trail. For many people, their service is more about the hikers than the physical aspect of the trail itself. This is especially true for trail angels who serve hikers year after year. Of course, many of these A.T. servants are not acting on foundations of faith. For them, it is part of the moral and ethical compass described by Einstein, or simply a desire to give back to something that has blessed them.

Some of the A.T. servants are overt in the cause of modeling their Christian faith by serving hikers. As St. Francis of Assisi said, *"Preach the gospel at all times. If necessary, use words."* I hope to be able to give back through regular service—and yet, here I just used words! – *"Mom"*

## Prayer

*"Father God, I long to hear your voice at the end of my life saying 'Well done, my good and faithful servant.' Please give me the opportunities to serve with all my heart, soul, and strength, so that I am a blessing to you and to those around me."*

In every person's life come moments of enlightenment—moments when one's understanding of where they are headed on their journey through life is turned completely upside-down. These same moments often challenge every belief one holds as to what is important and their perspective on the world in suddenly forced to take on an entirely new character.

Throughout our lives, we have heard lessons about humility, faith, perseverance, sacrifice, and service. However, it was not until our time on the Appalachian Trail, where we saw and experienced these lessons every day that we gained a new understanding and greater appreciation for what they truly meant. The lessons were everywhere and in everything and then, as we do now, we prayed for thanksgiving in all things.

Your moment of enlightenment may not come because of an event as dramatic as thru-hiking the Appalachian Trail, as it did for Mom and me. It may come during something as commonplace as driving to work or through the heart-wrenching trial of losing a loved one. For those who are seeking more to life, it is our sincere hope that the stories of our thru-hike, and the analogies presented between what we discovered during our life-changing journey and how they pertain to a walk of faith, have provided your moment of enlightenment. We also hope that you have found this book entertaining, thought-provoking and inspirational, and that it has opened a door for you to take that first step on your own life-changing journey—a journey of faith.

If what you have read in this book has been meaningful and has helped you to make a decision to become a Christian, perhaps you are wondering, *"Okay. Now what do I do next?"* Believe it or not, becoming a Christian is as easy as ABC.

"A" stands for **Admit**. Admit that you can not make it on your own and that you are aware that you have done and said things that, in your heart, you know were hurtful, immoral, shameful, unrighteous, corrupt, unprincipled, regretful, and just plain wrong. Admit these things to God, show sincere sorrow for your past behavior, and commit to not living that way in the future. This is the first step to receiving God's grace and forgiveness.

> *"...for all have sinned and fall short of the glory of God..."* - Romans 3:23 (NIV)

> *"Now it's time to change your ways! Turn to face God so he can wipe away your sins, pour out showers of blessing to refresh you..."* - Acts 3:19 (The Message)

> *"On the other hand, if we admit our sins—make a clean breast of them—he won't let us down; he'll be true to himself. He'll forgive our sins and purge us of all wrongdoing."* - 1 John 1:9 (The Message)

"**B**" stands for **Believe**. In order to be a Christian, you must believe that Jesus is God's Son and that God sent Jesus to earth to die in order to pay the penalty for everyone's sins. Read through the Bible and find a mentor or spiritual advisor who can walk you through the story of Jesus' life and explain to you how the plan of salvation works.

> *"For God so loved the world that he gave his one and only Son, that whoever believes in him shall not perish but have eternal life."* - John 3:16 (NIV)

> *"But God demonstrates his own love for us in this: While we were still sinners, Christ died for us."* - Romans 5:8 (NIV)

> *"For Christ died for sins once for all, the righteous for the unrighteous, to bring you to God. He was put to death in the body but made alive by the Spirit..."* - 1 Peter 3:18 (NIV)

"**C**" stands for **Confess**. Not only must you believe that Jesus is God's Son, you must also confess your faith in Jesus Christ as Savior and Lord. Confess, through prayer, that Jesus Christ is the only way to God and commit to live for Him the rest of your life.

> *"That if you confess with your mouth, "Jesus is Lord," and believe in your heart that God raised him from the dead, you will be saved. For it is with your heart that you believe and*

*are justified, and it is with your mouth that you confess and are saved."* – Romans 10:9-10 (NIV)

*"...for, "Everyone who calls on the name of the Lord will be saved."* - Romans 10:13

God loves every one of us and wants a personal relationship with each of us. But our desires, and our straying from the path He wants for us, keeps that from happening. Jesus Christ is the only answer to this problem. He's the only one who can bring us back to God. He is the "blaze" that guides our way on the trail that is a life of faith.

If you are wondering, *"Just how do I talk to God about turning my life over to Him,"* here is a short prayer that you can use.

*Dear Lord Jesus,*

*I know I have really messed up in life, I want to change, and I need your forgiveness. I believe that you died on the cross for my sins and rose from the grave to give me a new life. I know You are the only way to God, so help me stop living life my own way and help me start living for You. Please forgive me, change my life, and make yourself real to me.*

*In Jesus' name, Amen.*

Now, find a local church and let someone know about the decision that you've made. They will help you continue on your new journey, help keep you on the right "path" and help you reach the summit of your life in Christ.

For those who are already Christians, and understand the challenges and rich rewards of living a spirit-filled life, we hope that the devotional pieces provided solace and enrichment in those moments of solitude and reflection, either on the trail or in the comfort of your own home. May they help you to become increasingly grounded in your faith. We also hope that we have given you unique ways with which to explain what it means to be a Christian to those you meet who are searching for more to life in a context that they can be more readily understand and relate to.

If you are looking for additional, hiking-related insight into how to live a Christian life, we highly recommend, *Seeker's Guide to the Spiritual Wilderness*, by Craig & Suzy Miles. Their passionate stories about God's prominence and intervention during their days backpacking are inspirational and are useful as tools to use to reach out to people who you want to bring to Christ.

> *"I have walked many miles, have seen untold wonders, and have experienced unforeseen joy and hardship. There have been days bathed in sunlight and rainbows, and days when storms made my path near impossible to see. There were days when I stood among the clouds on a glorious, windy peak, gazing at all that lay ahead of me, and I fully understood why I was there and where I was heading.*
>
> *And then there were moments when the valleys I had to walk through, to reach that next mountaintop, were so deep and shrouded in shadows that I thought the valley may never end and I questioned my desire and ability to keeping going.*
>
> *But with each day, I held fast to my faith and continued to move forward, one small step at a time, knowing that ahead lay a reward beyond my comprehension."* - Windtalker

The God of Creation wants you to follow your dreams—the dreams that He gave to you to set your life on the His path. God has a plan for you and will use you, but you will need to put in the effort, just like we did when we pursued our dream of thru-hiking the A.T.!

> *"And we know that in all things God works for the good of those who love him, who have been called according to his purpose."* – Romans 8:28 (NIV)

Lest you think that you may be too old to pursue your dreams or begin your walk of faith, be assured that it is never too late. There is no timetable for dreams and God's timing for your life is always the correct timing.

*June 2$^{nd}$*

> *"...Our second night at the Dutch Haus B&B, in Montebello, Virginia, put us in contact with some new and old friends from the trail. At dinner that evening, we met "Baro" and*

*"Jangles" for the first time and there, as well,were our old friends, "Baldylocks," "Goldfish" and "Stumbles." The guest of honor at dinner that evening was "Wise Owl," an 80-year-old woman from Indiana, whose dream had always been to hike part of the Appalachian Trail. Through a unique non-profit organization called www.nevertoolate.org, she teamed up with a guide from www.webehiking.com, who planned and guided her through a five-day, forty-mile section of the trail. Her arrival for dinner hailed the completion of her dream. She entertained us with her ageless wisdom, subtle wit, and offbeat jokes, which were indicative of her feisty demeanor. She was presented with a certificate and an Appalachian Trial T-shirt to commemorate the completion of her dream. Through the raucous applause of all of us who were inspired by her accomplishment, tears welled up in "Mom's" and my eyes as we marveled at what the realization of her dream meant not only to her, but also to us. It was as if she had summited Katahdin with us and it was all the more special because of her age. For years, we had been telling ourselves and others, 'If you have a dream, never let not chasing it become a regret. Go after it with every ounce of your being, no matter what your age. Leave a legacy of being a Dream Chaser.' Being there for her award dinner reinforced our desire to continue doing just that."* –
Windtalker & Mom

What is interesting about this story is the effect that one person's dream can have on others. The organization, www.nevertoolate.org, was the dream of a gentleman by the name of Bob Haverstick. Bob is no stranger to meeting the needs of those around him and a large portion of his life has been spent in philanthropic endeavors. He was raised to believe that every man and woman, in his or her corner of the world, has a moral obligation to be a steward of his or her time, talent and money.

In early 1998, Bob, along with veteran radio producer Al Stone, began a radio program called "Heart-to-Heart" and from this program was born, "Never Too Late." "Never Too Late's" primary purpose is to reach out to people in nursing homes, assisted living facilities, hospice programs and adult day care facilities—regardless of age—and help make their dreams and wishes come true; sort of a "Make a Wish Foundation" for senior citizens.

*"Dream no small dreams for they have no power to move the hearts of men."* - Johann Wolfgang von Goethe

"Never Too Late's" secondary purpose is to honor requests from elder citizens (generally 65 and over), regardless of where they reside, providing they (or one of their family members) are willing to help.

As it turned out, Bob Haverstick's dream helped Wise Owl realize her dream, and through our chance meeting with her, and through the inspiration of other "dream chasers" like Bill Irwin, our dream of competing the Appalachian Trail took on new meaning and unmistakable significance. Immediately following the successful completion of our thru-hike, doors opened for us to share our adventure and all that we had learned. God had guided our dream and now He had set us on a new path—a path where we could use the faith lessons we learned from our Appalachian Trail thru-hike to provide others with a better understanding of His power and grace. Had we believed that because of our ages (56 and 47at the time) and our physical condition that our dream was out of reach, we would have never experienced the wonder He wanted us to experience. We would have also never found our special niche in His plan, nor would we have found the mission He had for our lives.

*"Twenty years from now you will be more disappointed by the things that you didn't do than by the ones you did do. So throw off the bowlines. Sail away from the safe harbor. Catch the trade winds in your sails. Explore. Dream. Discover."* - Mark Twain

All stories about "Windtalker" and "Mom's" 2006 Appalachian Trail thru-hike are taken from their book, *"Solemates, Lesson on Life, Love and Marriage from the Appalachian Trail"* or from their journals on www.trailjournals.com

*(3) Ben Reuschel* story used with permission of the Grand Rapids Press, Grand Raids, MI.

*(22) "When Prayers Are Not Answered: Finding Peace When God Seems Silent,"* by Elizabeth Rockwell, Copyright ©1999, by Hendrickson Publishers, Inc. ISBN: 1-56563-088-2. Used by permission. All rights reserved.

*(31,32) "All Things are Possible Through Prayer,"* Spire Books, Published by Jove Publications, Inc. for Fleming H. Revell Company. Copyright ©1978. Used by permission. All rights reserved.

*(20,21) "Praise Habit – Finding God in Sunsets and Sushi,"* David Crowder, Copyright ©2004, NavPress Publishing. ww.navpress.com. Used by permission. All rights reserved.

*(27) "The Heart of Worship Files,"* compiled by Matt Redman, Copyright ©2000, Gospel Light Ministries, Regal Publishing Group. Used by permission. All rights reserved.

*(12) Paul Abbott*, Senior Pastor, Cedarbrook Community Church, Clarksburg, Maryland. Used by permission. All rights reserved.

*(36,37,38) "Searching for God Knows What,"* Donald Miller, Copyright ©2004, Thomas Nelson Publishing, Inc., Nashville, TN. Reprinted by permission. All rights reserved.

*(16,23) "Glimpses of an Invisible God - Experiencing God in the Everyday Moments of Life,"* Copyright ©2003, Cook Communication Ministries, Honor Books. Used by permission. May not be further reproduced. All rights reserved.

*(19,30) "The Air I Breathe, Worship as a Way of Life,"* Lou Giglio, Copyright ©2003, WaterBrook Multnomah Publishing Group, a Division of Random House, Inc. Used by permission. All rights reserved.

**Georgia Harris** served in a leadership capacity at her former church and guided members of the church in discovering and using their God-given passions, gifts and talents in life, as well as ministry. She now teaches similar content at her current church where she and her husband also lead a marriage-focused small group.

She has a Masters Degree in Technical Management and is a physical scientist with the National Institute of Standards and Technology in Gaithersburg, Maryland. She is an internationally recognized authority on weights and measures and metrology education. She is also an avid photographer, and a small portion of the 5,300 photos she took along the Appalachian Trail are available online and on the DVD, *"Appalachian Trail Reflections."*

**Randy Motz** has served as a men's ministry director, head of a church sound team, worship team bassist and vocalist, a worship leader and currently leads a marriage-focused small group with his wife.

He is a composer, writer and performs live sound production work for concerts, corporate and civic events. He is also president of The Qualtech Resource Group, Inc., a multi-media creation company, as well as the driving force behind Windtalker Music, a music production company specializing in Native American flute music. In his spare time, he is the Supervisor of Activities for the Potomac Appalachian Trail Club.

Randy and Georgia reside in Germantown, Maryland.

# Other Media Resources from "Windtalker" & "Mom"

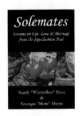

### "Solemates – Lessons on Life, Love & Marriage from the Appalachian Trail"

What happens when a middle-aged couple with no previous backpacking experience, decides to test their 14-year marriage and spend six months hiking the Appalachian Trail from Georgia to Maine in one continuous hike? Will their motto of *"Quitting is not an option"* be a blessing or a course?

Travel with "Windtalker" and "Mom," as they wrestle with their personal weaknesses and capitalize on each other's strengths, and in doing so, gain a deeper understanding of what it takes to make and keep a marriage strong.

"Solemates" is not a day-by-day journal of trail life but rather a candid, introspective and sometimes humorous look into the range of emotions experienced during the pursuit of such a life-changing adventure. It is a warmhearted account of lessons in perseverance, human nature, compassion, understanding, and teamwork. Their stories, and those of their thru-hiking companions, reveal insights into the human spirit and refreshing perspectives on what is truly important in life.

### "Appalachian Trail Reflections"

A fifty-minute, photographic diary DVD, composed of one-hundred-fifty images depicting the visual majesty and splendor of the Appalachian Trail as captured through the creative eye of photographer, and A.T. thru-hiker, Georgia "Mom" Harris.

Each photo is set against a soundtrack of soothing natural sounds and Native American flute composed and performed by her husband, and A.T. hiking partner, Randy "Windtalker" Motz.

Escape to the lofty, cloud swept mountains of Georgia, wander through the lush green forests of Shenandoah National Park, traverse the rugged ridgelines of New England and joyously summit the towering peak of Mt. Katahdin, as this DVD takes you on an awe-inspiring journey through the sights and sounds of the trail and through the changing seasons.

For those who have hiked the A.T., this DVD will take you back to those memorable days on the trail. For those who dream of hiking "A footpath for those who seek fellowship with the wilderness", it is a beautiful way to cultivate the inspiration to do so and to experience the ever-changing terrain that makes up this legendary trail.

## *"Windtalker – Native SoundScapes"*

The wonder, beauty and history of the Appalachian Trail are captured through the hauntingly majestic blend of Native American flute, piano, violin, orchestra and rock instrumentation.

Relax to acoustic "soundscapes" that take the listener on a musical journey into the heart and soul. Songs written and performed by Randy "Windtalker" Motz.

## *"Exploring the Appalachian Trail by RV, Sort Of..."*

For six months, Vince and Anita Hartigan cruised the highways and back roads from Springer Mountain, in Georgia to Mt. Katahdin in Maine, in their RV providing trail support to their daughter, a.k.a. "Mom" and her husband, a.k.a. "Windtalker" as they thru-hiked the famed Appalachian Trail.

*Exploring the Appalachian Trail by RV, Sort of..."* is not simply the story of their journey as "trail angels." It is also a comprehensive, illustrated atlas for those desiring to wander the byways along the A.T. and partake of the wonder and beauty that can be found there.

You will not only be inspired to pursue your own adventure along the Appalachian Trail but will be provided with,

- Detailed, full-color maps illustrating the routes traveled in order to rendezvous with "Windtalker" & "Mom;"
- Extensive information on, and reviews of, the many RV parks and campgrounds used;
- Secrets to make your own adventure more rewarding;

and many other tools to make your journey a memorable one.

Also available as a CD-ROM with active links to the many of the campgrounds and services mentioned in the book.

## *Appalachian Trail Photographs*

Adorn your walls with beautiful nature photos from the Appalachian Trail. Available in various sizes, matted or unmatted, these magnificent photos capture the mesmerizing beauty of the trail, from Georgia to Maine, and make wonderful gifts for the hiker or nature lover in your life. These photos are also available as note card sets.

All of these products are available at www.QualtechResourceGroup.com. Many of them are also available through other online retailers, at leading bookstores, the Appalachian Trail Conservancy, the Potomac Appalachian Trail Club, the Appalachian Mountain Club, Campmor, and from many outfitters along the A.T.

If you would like to read more about "Windtalker and Mom's" Appalachian Trail thru-hike, as well as their hike of The Long Trail, in Vermont, visit www.trailjournals.com/windtalkerandmom. You can also read journals about many of their other adventures at www.rmghadventures.com.

Randy and Georgia are also available for motivational, multi-media presentations about their A.T. thru-hike. If you are interested in having them speak to your organization, club, church or scout troop, contact them at qualtech.resource@verizon.net or, by phone, at 240-338-3816.

17686848R00082

Made in the USA
Charleston, SC
23 February 2013